LÜCHOW'S GERMAN COOKBOOK

Lüchow's German Cookbook

BY JAN MITCHELL

*The Story and the Favorite
Dishes of America's Most
Famous German Restaurant*

WITH AN INTRODUCTION AND ILLUSTRATIONS
BY LUDWIG BEMELMANS

Doubleday & Company, Inc., Garden City, New York

BIBLIOGRAPHICAL NOTE

First published . . . . October 30, 1952

  Second printing before publication

  Reprinted . . . . December 11, 1952
  Reprinted . . . . January 16, 1953
  Reprinted . . . . January 28, 1953
  Reprinted . . . . January 4, 1954
  Reprinted . . . . November 29, 1954
  Reprinted . . . . August 30, 1955
  Reprinted . . . . October 26, 1956
  Reprinted, Fifth Anniversary . . . . October 30, 1957
  Reprinted . . . . July 25, 1958
  Reprinted . . . . May 15, 1959
  Reprinted . . . . December 2, 1960
  Reprinted . . . . March 9, 1962
  Reprinted . . . . January 11, 1963
  Reprinted . . . . March 6, 1964
  Reprinted . . . . January 8, 1965
  Reprinted . . . . November 5, 1965
  Reprinted . . . . October 6, 1967
  Reprinted . . . . February 13, 1970
  Reprinted . . . . February 25, 1972
  Reprinted . . . . October 5, 1973
  Reprinted . . . . December 6, 1974
  Reprinted . . . . May 21, 1976

Library of Congress Catalog Card Number 52–5764

Down Where the Würzburger Flows, *copyright, 1902, by Harry Von
Tilzer Music Pub. Co. Copyright renewed, 1929, and assigned to Harry
Von Tilzer Music Pub. Co. Used by permission of copyright proprietor.*

ISBN: 0-385-06623-6
Copyright, 1952, by Leonard Jan Mitchell
*All rights reserved including the right to reproduce this book
or portions therefrom in any form.*
Printed in the United States of America
Designed by Alma Reese Cardi

To the Most Wonderful
People in the World—
My Patrons

CONTENTS

INTRODUCTION
BY LUDWIG
BEMELMANS

The German dictionary defines the word *"gemütlich"* as good-natured, jolly, agreeable, cheerful, hearty, simple and affectionate, full of feeling, comfortable, cozy, snug; and *"Gemütlichkeit"* as a state of mind, an easygoing disposition, good nature, geniality, pleasantness, a freedom from pecuniary or political cares, comfortableness.

Of the remaining few New York places that can call themselves restaurants, Lüchow's triumphs in *Gemütlichkeit*. This quality, strong as the handshake of an old friend and a slap on the shoulder, is nowhere more honest. It enfolds you as you enter into the agreeable paneled halls.

A fragrance, delicate, but not weak, and slightly male, rides the air. It composes itself of the aromas of solid cooking, of roast geese and ducks, of game and Huhn im Topf, of various things, sour and spicy, and tender cutlets simmering among *Steinpilze*.

Through it is wafted the bouquet of good wines, and above this hangs the blue cloud of the smoke of rare cigars. This obscures the stag and moose heads that are part of the décor, along with samples of the ironmonger's art.

The mood is supported by music equally enduring. The orchestra plays such aids to digestion as "Die Forelle" *von* Schubert, "The Tales of Hoffman," "William Tell," and "Silvia," and such romantic fare as "The Evening Star." Occasionally a belly laugh echoes through the "Nibelungen Ring," for Lüchow's clientele for the most part are an uninhibited and happy lot.

Every kind of restaurant finds its own public. Several of the best in New York have a patronage so select that they are checked into the premises with elaborate and embarrassing care, and seated according to a rigid protocol.

Mr. Seute, now vice-president of Lüchow's, but still functioning as the Herr Ober, is free of all the pretentiousness of his colleagues. He runs the restaurant, he directs traffic, and he places people with simple logic, where there is room. The doors are open and anyone is welcome. In the words of the venerable Mr. Seute: "You don't need a *gestarchte* shirt front to get in here. The only way you cannot come is *mitaus* a necktie."

It is as simple and as sound as this.

Along with the food, the authenticity of its atmosphere, it gives me restful ease, and has ever since I have been in America. I find it one of those places in which the mind hums in harmony with its surroundings. I have spent many pleasant hours there, engaged in leaning back and looking at the assemblage of people. There are the large parties who call themselves "Our Bunch" and from whom most of the belly laughs issue.

At other tables sit priests, students, national figures (the late Jules Bache was a regular Sunday-night client), diplomats, politicians with Italian friends in race-track suits with pearl stickpins in their neckties, theatrical folk with broad-shouldered blondes who have brought along Mama and Papa. It is alive with children and with dogs. It is the most kaleidoscopic restaurant in New York. Its waiters are the last of their kind, upstanding citizens, without a trace of servility in their make-up.

They are very busy people and sometimes serve you *mitaus* a napkin. Also, they are apt to hand you the menu upside down, and a moment after handing it to you, take it back again, mumbling, *"Der Sauerbraten is aus,"* and dramatically eliminate this delicacy from the menu with a bold stroke of a pencil stub, never longer than a smoked-out cigarette. They will then advise you about what's left in the kitchen, and also on anything else you want to know. It's a solid body of men, trustworthy and sound in the head. Their opinions are as definite as those of another race of philosophers, the New York taxi driver.

The only being, as yet, not in complete harmony with the establishment is Mr. Jan Mitchell, the new proprietor. He runs about the place with cautionary solicitude, worried lest he disturb anyone, much like a man whose wife lost a glove in a movie theater and forgotten where she sat. It is most curious that a modern man who looks as if he were in training for the winter Olympics should find his happiness in being the curator of a Goulash and Wiener Schnitzel Emporium, worrying about the consistency of Nudel Soup.

It is to be hoped that this one flaw will be corrected, that a steady diet of Kartoffelknödel, of Wienerschnitzel, and the greatest of the delights of Lüchow's, the Pfannkuchen mit Preisselbeeren, together with the proper amounts of the various beers and good wines, will pad his cheeks, round out his stomach, and put the roses on his nose.

We shall then no longer look at him with pity and suspicion, and, as we did recently, ask Mr. Seute, a man of proper weight, "Who is that man there?"

And Mr. Seute will not have to answer ashamedly behind his menu, as he did, "Oh, that one, *mitaus* der stomach, das ist der Boss."

Ludwig Bemelmans

THE
STORY
OF Lüchow's

"In a changing world, nothing changes at Lüchow's."

O. O. McIntyre, the beloved columnist, wrote these words twenty years ago, but they are as true today. Lüchow's has survived three wars, a major depression, Prohibition, and the complete transformation of its surroundings, and still it is a synonym for that gracious, generous, and leisurely hospitality which has all but disappeared from the harassed modern world.

For seventy years Lüchow's has imparted this hospitality, offering not only food and drink but the inner contentment that comes from enjoying such pleasures in an atmosphere of contentment, warm, friendly, satisfying both mind and body.

You may enter Lüchow's by either of the two doors in its baroque, dark brown exterior, which gazes with old-fashioned dignity upon the realities of Fourteenth Street. Once beyond these doors, the visitor enters into another world, where he will be as welcome as once were his father and grandfather.

The door on the right, toward Broadway and Union Square, leads into one of the few male refuges remaining in New York. In more prosaic circles it would be called the bar; at Lüchow's it has always been known as the Gentlemen's Grill. A man may eat or drink there, safe from the company of women, if that is his pleasure. If it is a seidel of Würzburger that pleases him, he will find himself confronting a vast mahogany stretch of bar, its mirrored expanse surmounted by hand carving brought to this country from Germany in the eighties, flanked by the crests of those Bavarian townships from which our beer is imported. At one end stands the knightly figure of Lohengrin, and at the other, on the wall, broods a shaggy buffalo head obtained at the St. Louis World's Fair in 1904. An oil painting of Bacchus appropriately surveys this scene from the opposite wall.

Lüchow's other entrance, for the family trade, leads directly into a small reception room, where a plaque advises you, "Through the doors of Lüchow's pass all the famous people of the world," a sentiment first expressed by James Montgomery Flagg, the artist. But these doors have also welcomed, as they always will, men and women from everywhere in the world who seek our hospitality.

They find it at once in the first room they enter, which parallels the bar but is completely walled from it. This front room, called simply "the restaurant," pre-dates August Lüchow, the founder himself. It has that nineteenth-century serenity, that air of high-ceilinged spaciousness which sets the tone of Lüchow's. To see its dark woods, the gas fixtures whose electric bulbs are a single concession to progress, and the leisurely diners is to witness a scene from the gracious past. Everywhere on the walls are reminders of it: oils by German and Dutch artists, a porcelain statue of Frederick the Great, and the first installment of an admirable collection of steins which line the walls of all the rooms. The intricate carving on these steins—scenes of hunting, battle, and religion—are reminders of the Lüchow heritage, which goes beyond its American beginnings to the spacious eating and drinking places of Munich and Hamburg, and the glories of the Rhine Valley.

One of these steins, a tall, graceful piece which holds six quarts, was presented to Lüchow's by the town of Würzburg, whose beer is our pride. It rests on the ledge which divides the "restaurant" room from the main rooms inside. The small space between, an anteroom with a narrow passage for customers, is decorated on one wall with photographs of the celebrities and their parties who have enjoyed our hospitality for so many years. This anteroom is also the headquarters of a vast, autocratic, yet genial gentleman, Ernst Seute, our maître d'hôtel.

Mr. Seute has a desk at the left, and from it he can see the pictures of those personages whom he has welcomed in his decades of service, or he can look out into those rooms where he presides at luncheon and dinner. He sits at the desk only a few hours out of the day, however. Most often he is waiting for you, beaming and benevolent, as you emerge into the main rooms. He has been at this post since 1912—the unofficial host of Fourteenth Street.

The ceilings are higher in these inner, main rooms, and the vistas are expansive. The anteroom, which we call the Hall of Fame, leads directly to the Garden through a fine hand-carved entrance. In the nineties, the Garden was literally that—an outdoor drinking salon in the German manner. Now its huge skylights suggest an indoor garden, and a mirror which nearly covers the east wall reflects its perennial gaiety. A large painting of Würzburg looks down upon the May wine bowls, a collection of Mettlach wine pitchers graces one shelf, and the steins are everywhere.

Only a lattice arrangement separates the Garden from the parallel Café, into which one comes from the street by way of the Gentlemen's Grill. Here, too, the scene is illuminated by the glass skylights done in the fifteenth-century style of Hans Sachs. Besides its stein collection, the Café is noted for its models of two of Columbus's ships, and an oil portrait of August Lüchow, in apparent satisfied contemplation of what has been done with his life's work.

The Café leads into, by means of a two-step elevation, the Hunt Room, where twenty-one mounted deer heads gaze in blank nonchalance upon the pleasant spectacle of their descendants being eaten with considerable satisfaction, and still further onward, toward Thirteenth Street, the Hunt Room opens into the Nibelungen Room, where Wagner's heroic figures float majestically about the upper borders in lush murals.

Similarly, on the other side, one moves from the Garden by the same two steps into the largest room of all, running parallel to the Nibelungen and Hunt rooms. We call this the New Room. It is only a little more than fifty years old.

The New Room is perhaps the most remarkable for several reasons. There at the entrance, for example, stands a splendid model of the four-masted *Great Republic,* launched by Donald McKay at East Boston on October 4, 1853, and burned a few weeks later at the pier in New York, where she was taking on cargo for her maiden voyage.

Art dominates the New Room. Small masterpieces of the Dutch, Austrian, and Flemish schools illuminate the walls, including an oil by Frans Snyders, one of Rubens' students, depicting a man with a bag of game. At the far end of the room is the prize of the collection, an enormous oil completely covering one wall, Auguste Hagborg's "October—The Potato Gathering." It covers the wall because August Lüchow bought it to fit the space; only later did he discover that the amorous eyes of museum curators were upon it.

Another reminder of Herr August is at the Garden end of the New Room—a mirror tipped between ceiling and entrance so that the proprietor, from his office upstairs, could see what customers were enjoying his food and awaiting his presence.

Oddly enough, if anything has changed at Lüchow's it is this same New Room. Once it was the stable attached to the place, and out of it rolled the heavy beer wagons, drawn by splendid horses, carrying barrels of Würzburger to other thirsty portions of the city. August Lüchow was its authorized New York distributor.

The site of our present kitchens was formerly occupied by

the Hubert Museum, which housed an assortment of wax figures and a few cages of wild animals. When the museum was vacating these premises to allow for the building of our new kitchens a lion escaped and stalked into the dining room, which was filled with patrons dining in a leisurely and sedate manner. Instantly the room was in a state of panic. Hoop skirts, which were the fashion of the day, did not deter the ladies from mounting the table nearest them. The sound of screams, accompanied by the crashing of china and glassware, and the sight of the flying hoop skirts so startled the lion that he turned, tail between his legs, and ran back into the museum. Some of the terror of the patrons could have been averted had they only known that the lion was so aged he had no teeth and had been fed for so many years on scraps from the Lüchow kitchen that a meal of human flesh was of no interest to him.

II

Lüchow's is more than a restaurant; it is a way of life. August Guido Lüchow, who created it, and whose mirror and portrait are now the only visible reminders of his expansive, happy personality, is still present in the spirit of the restaurant he founded, in its devotion to good living and good friends.

August was a Hanoverian who came to America in 1879, when he was in his early twenties, and went to work at once in Stewart's Saloon on Duane Street, where domestic beer and imported wines were the libations, and expensive oil paintings were the principal decoration.

He was there only a year before he came uptown to work as bartender and waiter for the Baron von Mehlbach, who operated a place dealing exclusively in beer. The future Lüchow's was then only an eighth of its present size. It ended far short of Thirteenth Street, where women of low repute congregated on the fringes of gay Fourteenth.

Young August had the ancient German virtue of thrift, and with the help of William Steinway, he was able within two years to buy out the Baron. He was only twenty-six. Almost at once his restaurant became the warmhearted, convivial capital of a Fourteenth Street world that is no more.

Union Square was the center of that world. It was not the crowded Square of proletarian oratory and Bowery backwash that we know today, but a quiet park with a great fountain at its center, lofty elms and maples shading it, and gas lamps illuminating its borders. On its west side were the fashionable shops of Tiffany, the Le Boutillier Brothers, Vantine's, Hearn's, Macy's, and Brentano's. On the east side was Dead Man's Curve, notorious as the worst traffic spot in America. There the cable cars came charging around the curve from Broadway into the Square, forced to travel at full speed and with the brakes released, or the cable grip would fail and the cars stop.

Fourteenth Street east of the Square was a happy succession of German beer halls and Italian wine gardens. August Lüchow was in good company with Lienau's, a beer house kept by a venerable German couple, and with Brubacher's Wine Garden, the Café Hungaria, the Alhambra Gardens, and all the other German, Austrian, and Hungarian places where beer was a nickel and a free lunch of pretzels, cheese, sausage, and pickles went with it.

Lüchow's place faced the five-block thoroughfare of Irving Place, where there were more luminaries of the theater, art, and literary worlds in residence than in any other neighborhood in the nation, perhaps in the world. Nearby was the Academy of Music, where Adelina Patti had made her debut in 1859, and Steinway Hall, where Rubinstein and Wieniawski were performing joint recitals in 1872. Around the corner was Tony Pastor's Theatre, in which Fritzi Scheff played "Mlle. Modiste" and had herself advertised on Lüchow's menus.

They all came to Lüchow's. There was gentle irony in James Huneker's famous line, "I took a walk and got as far as Lüchow's," remembering that on the day he wrote it he had taken up residence in the Morton House, at the corner of Broadway and Fourteenth Street. Huneker and Rafael Joseffy organized the Bohemian Club in a second-floor room of Lüchow's, and later the American Society of Composers, Authors and Publishers was formed in another room nearby.

Always Lüchow's was a favorite of musicians, long after Fourteenth Street ceased to be the center of New York's musical life. Rubinstein, Paderewski, and Caruso were often there, and De Pachmann, Richard Strauss, the De Reszkés, Ysaye, Zimbalist, Victor Herbert, and in later years, Toscanini. They listened with approval to the Vienna Art Quartette, an ageless ensemble whose personnel and number have changed with the years but which still plays, at the entrance of the New Room, everything from the lightest of classics to Wagner. Only jazz has never been heard in Lüchow's.

It was the temperamental musicians who created what may have been the only unpleasant incident in the history of the place. Huneker was sitting one night with August himself, Joseffy, De Pachmann, and others, when that tempestuous master of Chopin, De Pachmann, who admired no artist more than himself, called Joseffy an unprintable name, at which Huneker threw a seidel of beer in the pianist's face. Later in the evening, when the quarrel had been settled and the men were drinking again, Joseffy remarked reproachfully to Huneker, "And you, of all men, wasting such a lot of good beer!"

William Steinway was the restaurant's patron saint. He and his noted family entertained the great musicians of the world there, both in the downstairs room and in the private rooms upstairs, one of which is named for him. They were elegant affairs, not like the robust banquets given at Lüchow's by Diamond Jim Brady, where twenty ladies of the chorus, engaged as dinner companions for the guests, might find $500 and a diamond sunburst tucked under their napkins.

Mr. Steinway ate regularly at noon upstairs with his senior executives, where they consumed August's famed forty-five-cent luncheon. One day, on his way through the restaurant, he observed a very junior executive busily attacking his food, and coldly inquired, "How can you afford to eat here on your salary?" The interloper blushed, gulped, and never returned to Lüchow's until he was in the proper financial bracket.

As the distinguished head of an eminent firm, Mr. Steinway was not accustomed to being crossed, consequently he viewed with disapproval the day that August, endeavoring to keep up with rising costs, began the forty-five-cent luncheon with six oysters instead of the customary dozen. He announced that he would take his trade elsewhere, and for a few days he did not appear. August was not worried. Mr. Steinway came back within a week and made no further complaints. Six or a dozen, there was still no place like Lüchow's.

They came year after year to enjoy it, generation after generation, the musicians, writers, artists, actors and actresses, the politicians and the financiers—O. Henry, H. L. Mencken, George Jean Nathan, Lillian Russell, Anna Held, Al Smith, Dudley Field Malone, Theodore Dreiser, Charles F. Murphy and the sachems of Tammany Hall, Theodore Roosevelt (from Police Commissioner of New York to President), Mack Sennett, who originated the name of his Keystone Comedies there one summer day at luncheon in 1912; and Gus Kahn, who penned, "Yes, Sir, That's My Baby" on a tablecloth.

Every evening was a gala occasion, every Sunday night a festival. Victor Herbert brought back an eight-piece orchestra from Vienna, which he conducted for nearly four years. Brady's Parties were more than matched by the dinners of Jules Bache, Andrew Carnegie, and J. P. Morgan, which made culinary history. The three-hour lunch was commonplace, and the whole evening was devoted to dining.

Lüchow's became the American agent for Würzburger beer in 1885, and for Pilsner soon after. August was not the first man to serve these fine imported beers in America, but he was first to make them popular, a fact attested by the popular classic

Harry von Tilzer wrote to honor August and his restaurant, "Down Where the Würzburger Flows," whose lyrics by Vincent Bryan proclaimed:

> *Rhine wine it is fine,*
> *But a big stein for mine,*
> *Down where the Würzburger flows!**

The song traveled from Fourteenth Street to the beer gardens of Cincinnati, St. Louis, Chicago, Milwaukee, and far beyond, and attained such popularity that August declared in some bewilderment: "I feel like a kind of beer Columbus!"

But Lüchow also was a connoisseur of wines, and from Europe he brought back a cellar to be proud of, from Forster Jesuitengarten, Rudesheimer Berg and Niersteiner; from Laubenheimer at $1.50 a quart, to Steinberger Trockenbeer at $25 a quart. August never permitted hard liquor to be served at the tables, although it could be had at the bar. Brandy after dinner was an exception. August liked it.

Of the trenchermen who ate and drank at Lüchow's, the Baron Ferdinand Sinzig, of the House of Steinway, established a record which still stands by downing thirty-six seidels of Würzburger—without rising. Envious competitors observed that he was a native of Cologne and therefore presumably without kidneys.

Sometimes the gaiety and good will of the place overflowed its boundaries. On March 11, 1902, when the younger brother of the last Kaiser, Prince Henry of Prussia, and his entourage had completed a sentimental tour of the country and were ready to sail, August Lüchow was reluctant to let him go without a gesture of farewell. The gesture consisted of chartering a river steamer, which took on an impressive cargo of beer and wine, bales of frankfurters, gallons of sauerkraut, a German band, and everybody who wanted to see the Prince off. In a fine glow of gastronomy and alcohol, the little ship clung to the stern of Henry's liner as she sailed eastward, its passengers shrieking bon voyages into her wake long after she had disappeared. No one who was present ever forgot the voyage, but no one could recall how it ended.

Beer, wine, food, music, and atmosphere—all these contributed to the success of Lüchow's, but without August it would have had no meaning. The stories of this big, good-natured, handle-bar-mustachioed man are innumerable. One of the most characteristic concerns the day long ago when Lüchow's had its only labor trouble, a brief strike of waiters. The walkout enraged August, who had always treated his waiters as though they were his children. On the day of the strike he stalked about the restaurant, serving the customers himself and giving everyone a pancake loaded with caviar—as one who saw it remarked, "a gesture of generosity born of rage."

Often I imagine I see him now, moving amiably from table to table, greeting his friends, his laugh resounding in the rooms, eating and drinking with a zeal unequaled by any of his customers. No one enjoyed Lüchow's more than August Lüchow. Early in the morning, when the last guests had departed, he was sometimes so heavy with food and beer that four busboys had to assist him up the stairway to the rooms where he lived with his sister.

August never married. His loves were his restaurant and his friends.

III

It is a tribute to Lüchow's that it survived Prohibition. The drought had settled firmly by 1923, when August died, and Victor Eckstein, a nephew-in-law of Mr. Lüchow, who succeeded him as proprietor, had to rely upon food and tradition to carry him over the dry years.

No one pretends that this was a happy period in the restaurant's existence, but the faithful returned night after night for the excellent dinners, and possibly to mourn the Würzburger which flowed no more. The orchestra still played its nostalgic repertoire, an island in a sea of jazz, and the atmosphere of dignified pleasure remained unchanged.

During the last four or five years of Prohibition, Lüchow's did not celebrate New Year's. For a time it had tried to keep up this tradition, which had always been such a gay time, but the customers who brought their flasks so desecrated the atmosphere that Mr. Eckstein concluded it would be wiser to wait for repeal. His reward was café license number one in New York City, given to Lüchow's for its "excellent record," when beer started flowing again.

On that joyous May day in 1933, a thousand people came to dinner, and during the festivities consumed eight half barrels of Würzburger, which is equivalent to a thousand seidels. It was by no means a record. In the old days, Lüchow's imported seventy thousand half barrels of German beer annually, equal to a consumption of twenty-four thousand seidels a day.

It is this same Würzburger which remains as one of the unchanging delights of Lüchow's. It is perhaps the most reliable accompaniment to the glories of the German cuisine which were and are our stock in trade. The details of that cuisine are abundantly reviewed in the pages that follow. It ranges from the reliables, like pig's knuckles and sauerkraut, the various kinds of schnitzel, and the things our chefs do with veal and potato dumplings, to goose and duck and game. We can provide such delicacies as turtle flippers à la Maryland, or a staple like a beefsteak dinner, which at Lüchow's begins with oysters Rockefeller, goes on with onion soup, continues with a double lamb chop, a delectable prelude to the steak itself, and concludes with Swiss cheese.

The customers, like the menu, have changed very little in seventy years. Composers like Victor Herbert have been succeeded by Irving Berlin and Richard Rodgers; the singers of the Golden Age by such opera stars of today as Helen Traubel; literary figures of the twenties like Theodore Dreiser by best-selling authors of today—Thomas B. Costain, Bob Considine, Kenneth Roberts, John P. Marquand, and a host of others.

Always these celebrities have their favorite Lüchow stories. Ted Husing, the noted sports announcer and disk jockey, has one that goes all the way back to his father's memories of Lüchow's. Of course this memory was a very special one, not easily forgotten. Husing, Sr., his son recalls, knew that if a young man invited a girl to Sunday dinner at Lüchow's it was virtually a declaration of his intentions, consequently it was a serious day in his life when he arrived in a rented hack to take the girl he married to the restaurant that was even then famous, more than a half century ago. He waited until dessert to make his proposal, because that was the proper etiquette. Then, red-faced in his high, stiff collar, he blurted: "I hope you enjoyed the dinner, and I hope you don't mind my not kneeling, but if you've finished your pancake—would you marry me?"

Much more recently, a tour of our resplendent beer list was conducted one hot summer night by Charles Morton, the author of numerous civilized essays, who is also the *Atlantic Monthly's* perceptive associate editor.

The evening began in Boston, where a few hours earlier Mr. Morton and a friend had decided to drive down to New York in a supercharged Ford, of which the editor was exceedingly fond. They departed about five in the afternoon, and an equal number of hours later found themselves bowling along the West Side Highway into a city that appeared deserted and from whose still streets the heat shimmered even at that hour.

Lüchow's was cool and wonderfully tranquil, a veritable oasis. At the time there were a dozen or so draught German beers on the card, and the Bostonians decided that the only fair thing would be to tour right through the list. Mr. Morton's beer-drinking philosophy is that the only way to make a decent comparison of beer is to sample one brew while the full sense of another has just been attained. He was astonished at the delicate variations which were so unmistakably transmitted to the palate—all different and all excellent.

Morton and his friend made two complete trips through our list and were comfortably engaged on a third when they mercifully permitted the bartender to go home. It was, says the *Atlantic's* man, the most satisfactory beer-tasting he ever attended.

On occasion the Lüchow cuisine has been known to impress even a Hollywood agent. One of this breed, who fancied himself as a gourmet of formidable standards, once took Jerome Weidman, the best-selling novelist, for lunch at the restaurant. It was Weidman's first experience, and his host had spent some time describing its wonders. "But I insist on ordering for both of us," said the Hollywood Escoffier.

The first dish came in a large tureen. The host ladled some into his plate, tasted it, and expressions of violent rapture soared into Lüchow's serene noontime air. It was an extraordinary performance, worthy of an Academy Award. He waved his hands, kissed his fingertips to the ceiling, gurgled happily, and went on sipping.

At last he insisted on sending for the chef, who appeared and witnessed a reprise of the performance with some astonishment. The chef took the compliment gracefully and retired to the kitchen. Weidman's host insisted on walking him back, as a mark of gratitude. When they had gone, the writer ladled a bit of the tureen's contents into his own plate and took a tentative sip. It was good. Looking up, he saw a waiter standing at his elbow. Weidman didn't know whether he was expected to repeat his host's performance or not, but obviously the waiter was expecting something.

He took another sip and asked, "What is it?"

"Soup," the waiter remarked succinctly, and walked away.

Lüchow's chefs have always been accustomed to dealing directly with the customers on occasion, but no one except Diamond Jim Brady would have thought to bring his own cook to the restaurant with a request that the chef give her his recipe for a favorite Brady dish. Obligingly he wrote it out and, handing it to the cook, explained, "This recipe does for fifty servings."

"Thank you," the cook responded, and added approvingly, "Then I won't have to change it for Mr. Brady."

To return to modern instances, Sigmund Spaeth, widely known as the "Tune Detective," who writes, lectures, and broadcasts about music, enjoys another activity not so well publicized. He has the habit of eating off other people's plates. It is, he asserts, a real mark of affection on his part.

One night at Lüchow's, Dr. Spaeth was sitting beside the late Beatrice Kaufman, wife of the playwright George S. Kaufman. When the waiter brought her vanilla ice cream for dessert, Dr. Spaeth inquired indignantly, "How can you order vanilla when you know I like chocolate?"

Mrs. Spaeth recalls another time at Lüchow's when she was eating an artichoke, while her husband kept pace with her in pulling off the leaves. He interrupted himself to ask politely, "I'm not hurrying you, am I?"

To me Lüchow's is like home. The kitchen and its workings have had a compelling magic for me since I was a little boy. My first memory is being in our vast kitchen, observing the huge stove and even larger bake oven. Always the preparation and service of food at our homes in Sweden and on the Baltic, often for large hunting parties, fascinated me. Many times I used my piggy-bank savings to buy presents for our cooks, in gratitude for letting me help prepare roasts, sauces, pastries, and breads.

Nevertheless, I was headed for a country squire's life until 1932, when I saw Lüchow's on my first visit to the United States. I fell in love with its atmosphere, tradition, and fine food—it all reminded me of home. From that day, my chief desire was to own this famous old hostelry.

Back home again, I told my family that I desired to learn the restaurant business, and so, after completing my studies at the University of Stockholm, I attended a school of hotel management in Zurich. Returning to America in 1940, determined to make this country my home, I bought an old established restaurant in Washington, D.C. It was successful, but still I longed for Lüchow's. For five years I traveled frequently to New York, trying to persuade Mr. Eckstein to sell it to me. When I had convinced him that I would preserve the atmosphere and traditions of the place, he consented.

In buying Lüchow's it was my object to bring back the splendor of the old days, as well as to preserve what remained of them. Especially I wanted to bring back the festivals—the Venison Festival, the Goose Feast, the Bock Beer Festival, and the May Wine Festival, with beer served in the old beer mugs, replicas of the menus of 1900, German bands playing, and all the rest that memory recalls. One of my rewards has been the heartwarming appreciation of the patrons who have thanked me for preserving one of the few New York landmarks that survive.

But a more personal satisfaction comes especially at Christmas time, when the largest indoor tree in the city towers twenty-five feet or more in the Café, aglow with five hundred electric candles and original nineteenth-century toys imported from Germany. The holy village is beneath, with the church bells chiming hymns and the Apostles revolving in the tower, all hand-carved by famous woodcarvers in Oberammergau, Bavaria, and the orchestra plays carols while the diners sing. Some of these diners have been coming for a half century, and the waiters who serve them did so when they both were young. Nor has the Christmas menu changed, with its oxtail soup, boiled carp, roast goose with chestnut stuffing, creamed onions, pumpernickel, plum pudding with brandy sauce, and ice cream Santa Clauses.

And when the lights are turned down at six o'clock on Christmas Eve, the orchestra plays "Silent Night," and the tree blazes suddenly with its own special glory, the true reward comes to me. The old friends of August Lüchow shake my hand, often with the tears on their cheeks, and they say to me, "If August should come in tonight, he would feel at home. Nothing has been changed."

—J. M.

HOW WE COOK AT Lüchow's

1.

APPETIZERS

Old hands who have been eating at Lüchow's for more years than they can readily remember have developed a capacity which does not shrink at the generosity of the restaurant's appetizers. The uninitiated, however, thinking to nibble at a modest beginning to a hearty meal are likely to find themselves overwhelmed by a small mountain of herring salad, a substantial plate of head cheese covered with a special vinaigrette sauce, or some other dish which dampens their enthusiasm for whatever follows. Be warned, then. Unless you are a trencherman of proved capacity, deal humbly with the appetizers.

What is true of the appetizers is true also of the entire menu. Mr. Seute's philosophy is that old customers should have the best and new ones the same, consequently everyone gets the ample portions which have filled and satisfied Lüchow's patrons for seventy years.

It takes twenty-eight cooks, masters from Austria and South Germany, some of them in Lüchow service for thirty-five years, to produce the Lüchow cuisine. None of these cooks would dream of modifying or changing the traditional European recipes which are as much a part of the restaurant as Mr. Seute himself.

PICKLED BEEF HEAD SALAD
OCHSENMAUL SALAT

> *10 pounds fresh boned beef heads*
> *1 fresh veal knuckle*
> *3 onions*
> *5 bay leaves*
> *1 dozen cloves*
> *1 bunch fresh thyme*
> > (*Put bay leaves, cloves, and thyme in cheese-cloth, tie. Remove when cooked.*)

Marinate beef heads in water, salt, and saltpeter for one week.

Place corned beef heads with fresh veal knuckle in water. Add remaining ingredients and boil about 4 hours. Remove veal bones. Press beef heads between two pans. Cool; cut in julienne. Marinate in olive oil, wine vinegar, chopped onions, freshly ground pepper.

Serve chilled on crisp lettuce with finely cut chives. Serves 8–10.

PIG'S HEAD CHEESE VINAIGRETTE

> *1 pig's head (without cheeks), boned*
> *1 cup salt*
> *½ cup sugar*
> *½ tablespoon saltpeter*
> *2 quarts water*
> *Bag of spice (4 or 5 peppercorns, bay leaf, sprig of thyme, teaspoon allspice)*
> *1 teaspoon paprika*
> *½ teaspoon cayenne*

Scrub pig's head thoroughly. Rinse, drain, and cover with cold water to which 2 or 3 tablespoons salt have been added. Cover; let stand in refrigerator overnight.

Drain, rinse, cover with fresh water, and let stand 1 hour. Drain again. Place pig's head in an enamel kettle; add ½ cup salt, the sugar, saltpeter, and 2 quarts water. Cover kettle and let stand 5 days in refrigerator.

Remove pig's head from liquid; rinse. Place in a kettle; cover with fresh water; add spice bag. Bring to a boil, then lower heat and let cook slowly until meat drops from the bones. Remove spice bag; take kettle from heat. Remove all bones from meat; dice meat; add paprika and cayenne. Before meat is cold, press it into mold or pan 2 or 3 inches deep. Barely cover it with broth in which meat cooked. Let cool thoroughly. Slice and serve with special Lüchow Vinaigrette Sauce. (See recipe.) Serves 8.

CALF'S HEAD CHEESE VINAIGRETTE

> *1 calf's head*
> *1 beef head*
> *2 gallons water*
> *½ pound salt*
> *1 tablespoon saltpeter*
> *1 bay leaf*
> *6 cloves*
> *6 peppercorns*
> *½ teaspoon dried sage*
> *1 cup wine vinegar*
> *¼ cup oil*
> *½ teaspoon coarsely ground black pepper*
> *2 onions, chopped*
> *2 tablespoons minced chives*

Have butcher bone heads, remove eyes, brains, ears, snout,

and most of fat. Soak heads in cold water to extract blood. Wash, drain, and place in a large crock. Cover with 2½ gallons water; add salt and saltpeter. Let stand in cold place 10 days.

Drain, rinse, cover with cold water, and bring to boil. Lower heat; add bay leaf, cloves, peppercorns, and sage. Let simmer about 5 hours. Pour meat and stock into mold or pan; let cool. When stock has jelled firmly, cut in narrow strips.

Mix vinegar, oil, pepper, and onions; pour over head cheese. Garnish with chives. Serves 6 or more.

HERRING APPETIZER
HERING SALAT

> 4 salt herrings
> 6 boiled potatoes
> 3 apples
> 4 sour dill pickles
> 2 cooked beets
> Boiled veal knuckle
> 1 green pepper
> ½ onion
> Dash of black pepper
> 1 teaspoon sugar
> ½ teaspoon dry mustard
> ½ cup olive oil
> ½ cup wine vinegar
> 1 cup stock or bouillon
> 6 fresh lettuce leaves
> 3 tablespoons capers
> 3 hard-cooked eggs

Rinse herrings; drain; cover with cold water and let soak overnight. Drain; remove skin; cut fillets from bones. Dice fillets fine.

Peel and dice potatoes; peel, core, and dice apples; dice pickles, beets, meat, green pepper, and onion. Combine all with fish in a shallow dish. Sprinkle with pepper, sugar, and mustard. Pour oil, vinegar, and stock over all. Cover and let chill in refrigerator.

Serve on crisp lettuce garnished with capers and hard-cooked egg quarters or slices. Serves 6.

MARINATED HERRING

> *24 herring fillets*
> *1 quart sour cream*
> *1 cup vinegar*
> *2 tablespoons olive oil*
> *6 medium-size onions, sliced*
> *3 sour apples, peeled and cut in thin strips*
> *1 ounce peppercorns*
> *1 ounce bay leaves*
> *½ lemon, sliced thin*

Wash fillets; drain; arrange in bowl. Mix all other ingredients; pour over herring. Cover and place in refrigerator. Let chill and marinate 24 hours. Serves 24.

HERRINGS IN WINE SAUCE

> *8 salt herrings*
> *1 cup prepared mustard*
> *1 cup olive oil*
> *Juice 1 lemon*
> *½ cup dry white wine*
> *Dash ground black pepper*
> *2 tablespoons sugar*
> *Crisp lettuce*

Rinse herrings; drain; cover with cold water and let soak overnight. Drain; remove skin; cut fillets from bones; discard skin
and bones. Cut fillets in 2-inch lengths, or serving-size pieces.
Combine all other ingredients and pour over herrings in a
bowl. Cover bowl and let stand in refrigerator to chill and
marinate. Serve with garnish of crisp lettuce. Serves 10 or more.

Herrings in Mustard Sauce: Use ½ cup prepared mustard;
omit wine; add 4 tablespoons wine vinegar. Combine and use
with other ingredients as described.

HERRING IN DILL SAUCE

> *8 fresh herrings (6 to the pound)*
> *Salt*
> *1 cup prepared mustard*
> *1 cup olive oil*
> *4 tablespoons vinegar*
> *Juice 1 lemon*
> *1 cup coarsely chopped fresh dill*
> *½ tablespoon coarsely ground black pepper*
> *¼ tablespoon white pepper*
> *½ tablespoon salt*
> *½ tablespoon whole allspice*
> *2 tablespoons sugar*

Clean herrings; remove skin and cut fillets from bones; discard
bones. Rinse fillets; pat dry; sprinkle with salt.

Combine mustard and oil and beat smoothly until mixture
has the consistency of mayonnaise; add vinegar gradually, beating well, then lemon juice and remaining ingredients. If necessary, thin with a little water; or if vinegar is mild, thin mixture
with additional vinegar.

Place herring fillets in a deep platter or dish; pour mixture
over them and let stand, covered, in refrigerator 3 or 4 days, or

until fish is well flavored with the sauce. Garnish with thinly sliced red onions and sprig of fresh dill. Serves 8 or more.

This was the favorite appetizer of Frederick Augustus III, the last King of Saxony. Oscar Hofmann was his chef. August Lüchow, on a trip to Germany, was entertained at the royal household. He liked the cooking so much that, with the King's consent, he persuaded Hofmann to come to America with him and made him the chef at his restaurant. The Herring in Dill Sauce is one of the recipes he brought with him.

LÜCHOW'S SPECIAL APPETIZER
DELIKATESSE KALTER AUFSCHNITT

> *Sliced cold assorted wursts*
> *Sliced head cheese*
> *Fancy bolognas*
> *Cervelat*
> *Homemade liverwurst*
> *Dill pickles*
> *Olives*
> *Celery hearts*
> *Radishes*
> *Sardines*
> *Herring in Sour Cream*
> *Mayonnaise*
> *Mustard*
> *Vinaigrette Sauce*

An assortment of cold sausages or wursts is served garnished with pickles, olives, sliced radishes, and celery hearts. If head cheese is in the assortment, one of Lüchow's special vinaigrette sauces for head cheese (see recipes) is served with the condiments.

HOMEMADE CHICKEN LIVER PÂTÉ

½ pound onions, sliced
½ cup goose or chicken fat
½ cup chicken stock or bouillon
1 pound fresh pork liver
2 pounds chicken livers
¾ pound fat salt pork cut in thin strips
1 teaspoon salt
½ teaspoon pepper
3 cloves
⅛ teaspoon thyme
1 bay leaf, crumbled
3 eggs, beaten
1 cup heavy cream
1 cup sherry wine
2 tablespoons cornstarch
2 tablespoons butter

Cook onions in goose or chicken fat with stock until they are transparent and tender.

Wash liver; drain; lard with strips of salt pork, then slice liver into saucepan. Add onions, the fat they cooked in, salt, pepper, cloves, thyme, and bay leaf. Cover with cold water. Cook slowly (simmer) in covered pan until all blood is withdrawn and liver is very tender, about 2 hours. Drain.

Grind liver and cooked onions fine. Mix with eggs, cream, and most of the wine. Moisten cornstarch smoothly with remaining wine and beat into the liver mixture. Beat and mix to a smooth paste. Pack into a crock or mold; pour 2 tablespoons melted butter over the top. Keep covered in the refrigerator. To serve, cut in slices. Serves 10 or more.

Variation: Add 2 or 3 chopped anchovies or finely minced truffles to the pâté for variations in flavor.

Famous patrons of Lüchow's, in the days when good dining

was more important than a waistline, ordered a superb wine with this pâté. The recommended wine is a white, still wine, a Josephshofer Auslese, a select dry Moselle from the hills outside Trier. It is served expertly chilled.

PICKLED MUSHROOMS

This is a Lüchow favorite as a first course, with other appetizers such as pâté, head cheese, or smoked eel.

To make Pickled Mushrooms in the traditional German way, buy fresh button mushrooms; use only firm, white ones.

1 pound small button mushrooms
1 tablespoon salt
1 medium-size onion, chopped fine
1 clove garlic
¼ cup chopped fresh parsley
2 bay leaves
4 coarsely ground peppercorns
½ teaspoon crumbled dried thyme or chopped fresh thyme
2 cups dry white wine
2 cups cider vinegar
½ cup olive oil
Juice ½ lemon

Wash mushrooms thoroughly in cold water containing 1 tablespoon salt. Drain.

Mix all other ingredients; pour over mushrooms in an enameled saucepan. Bring to a boil, then let simmer 8 to 10 minutes or until tender. Let cool. Keep covered in refrigerator, seal while hot in sterile glass jars. Makes 6 large servings. Serves 8 or more small servings.

2.

SOUPS

It was a wise gourmet who first propounded the old gastronomic axiom that a fine restaurant may best be judged by its soups. For the chef who is charged with preparing soup has assumed a grave responsibility. His creation must be weighty enough to satisfy but light enough not to diminish enthusiasm for what follows. It must be a graceful salute to the diner's appetite, a subtle compliment to his taste.

Here at Lüchow's we treat the making of soup with the respect it deserves. Naturally, the ingredients must be of the finest. The beef, for example, which goes into Kraft Suppe, the Double Consommé with Beef and Vegetables, and similar concoctions, is purchased with as much care as we devote to steaks, fish, or game. The vegetables, too, must be of a quality as high as though they were to be offered by themselves.

The small miracle of excellent soup is not accomplished with ingredients alone, however, since one must suppose that any good chef begins with the proper equipment. What distinguishes soup is the skill of mixture, the delicate and difficult addition of seasonings, until the chef's experienced palate tells him at last that the point of perfection has been reached. Then, and only then, does he pronounce it ready for Lüchow's tables.

DOUBLE CONSOMMÉ WITH BEEF AND VEGETABLES
SUPPENTOPF

> *3 pounds beef*
> *1 pound soup bones*
> *1½ teaspoons salt*
> *4 quarts water*
> *½ small onion*
> *½ small carrot*
> *1 stalk celery*
> *1 small piece kohlrabi*
> *1 small piece parsley*
> *1 tomato, quartered*
> *Boiled vegetables such as 3 or 4 small potatoes,*
> *6 small carrots, and 3 or 4 small turnips*

Wipe meat with wet cloth. Rinse bones and place in kettle with salt, vegetables, and water. Bring slowly to a boil, then boil 1 hour. Skim top. Add beef. Cover and let boil slowly 2½ to 3 hours. Lift meat out and place in deep tureen; keep meat warm. Strain stock, reheat. Pour over meat and cooked hot vegetables. Serves 6.

LENTILS WITH BAUERNWURST
LINSEN SUPPE

> *2 cups dried lentils*
> *3 quarts bouillon or stock*
> *Ham knuckle, or ¼ pound salt pork (1 piece)*
> *3 small potatoes, diced*
> *1 tablespoon butter*
> *1 teaspoon flour*
> *1 bauernwurst*

Wash lentils; drain. Cover with cold water and let soak 1 hour. Drain. Cover with cold water again and bring to a boil. Boil 10 minutes. Drain again. Add bouillon or stock and ham knuckle or piece of salt pork. Bring to a boil. Lower heat and cook slowly 2½ to 3 hours.

Twenty minutes before lentils are done, add potatoes. Mix butter and flour. Stir this into the mixture. Continue to boil a few minutes.

Simmer wurst 10 minutes in barely enough water to cover. Drain. Slice into tureen or soup plates. Pour hot lentils over sausage and serve. Serves 6.

BEEF SOUP WITH MARROW
KRAFT SUPPE

> *1 pound short rib beef*
> *3 quarts water*
> *1 teaspoon salt*
> *½ teaspoon pepper*
> *1 leek*
> *1 stalk celery*
> *2 medium-size carrots, diced*
> *½ potato, diced*
> *16 small slices raw beef marrow*
> *¼ cup minced chives*

Cover meat with water and bring to a boil. Skim the top, then drain the meat. Cover with 3 quarts water; add seasonings and all vegetables except potato. Bring to a boil. Lower heat; cover; simmer 1½ hours. Add potato; boil 1 hour longer. Serve with 2 slices raw beef marrow, garnished with a few chives, in each soup plate. Serves 8.

> *Kraft Suppe was a favorite with Arthur Brisbane, for many years famous editor and columnist of the Hearst papers. He ate it from the large silver cups in*

*which it was carried from the kitchen, rather than have
it served into soup plates at the table. A man of strong
ideas, he was adamant about eating his soup hot.*

BARLEY SOUP WITH GIBLETS
GRAUPENSUPPE MIT HÜHNERKLEIN

> *1 cup pearl barley*
> *Boiling water*
> *1 tablespoon butter*
> *2 quarts beef or chicken bouillon*
> *2 cups broth in which giblets cooked*
> *¼ teaspoon grated nutmeg*
> *Chopped chicken giblets*
> *Salt and pepper*
> *2 tablespoons chopped parsley*

Wash barley; drain. Pour boiling water over it twice and drain.
Heat butter; cook barley 2 or 3 minutes. Place barley, boullion,
broth from giblets, and nutmeg in soup kettle. Boil slowly 1½
hours. Add giblets for last 20 minutes of cooking. If seasoning
is needed, add salt and pepper. Add parsley before serving.
Serves 6.

COOKED GIBLETS:

> *Chicken giblets*
> *1 cup white wine*
> *1½ cups chicken stock or bouillon*
> *½ teaspoon salt*
> *¼ teaspoon pepper*
> *¼ teaspoon grated nutmeg*

Wash giblets; drain; split and clean gizzard. Add wine, stock,
and seasonings. Cover and cook slowly until all are tender, 20
minutes or longer. Drain; chop giblets. Save liquid and use as
described above.

VENISON SOUP
ST. HUBERTUS OR WILDBRET SUPPE

> *1 shoulder venison, boned*
> *Salt*
> *2 tablespoons butter*
> *2 tablespoons flour*
> *¼ cup sausage meat*
> *1 partridge, cleaned, dressed, and boned*
> *2 slices lean bacon*
> *4 carrots, chopped*
> *2 onions, chopped*
> *2 leeks, chopped*
> *2 sprigs parsley*
> *½ teaspoon thyme*
> *1 bay leaf*
> *2 cups water*
> *2 or 3 cups stock or bouillon*
> *Toast triangles*
> *Seasoning*

Cut venison in large pieces, season with salt, and dredge with flour. Brown meat in butter on all sides. Place venison in soup kettle or soup casserole. Add water to cover. Cook slowly for about 50 minutes.

Rinse partridge inside and out; pat dry. Fill with sausage meat; skewer opening tightly with toothpicks. Cut bacon in small pieces and heat in frying pan. Cook partridge and vegetables in fat until golden and tender. Add herbs and water. Cover pan; simmer 10 minutes.

Add vegetables, partridge, and liquid in which they cooked to venison kettle. Cover and let boil gently 25 minutes. Skim top. Lower heat and let simmer 2 hours.

When venison is done, place in a warmed soup tureen and

keep hot. Remove partridge and take sausage stuffing out of it. Chop or grind partridge. Mix stuffing and partridge; season with salt and pepper if needed; spread on toast triangles to serve with soup.

Strain soup. Add bouillon as needed to make 6 large servings. Reheat. Pour over venison in tureen. Serves 6.

CREAM OF CHICKEN SOUP
SUPPE, HEIDELBERGER ART

> *1 quart beef stock or bouillon*
> *2 cups water*
> *1 teaspoon sugar*
> *2 tablespoons rice or barley*
> *3- to 4-pound chicken, cleaned and dressed*
> *1 tablespoon salt*
> *1½ tablespoons butter or chicken fat*
> *1 tablespoon flour*
> *1¼ cups cream*
> *3 egg yolks, beaten*

Combine stock or bouillon and water in large kettle; add sugar and rice or barley.

Rinse chicken; drain; pat dry. Rub lightly with salt. Place chicken in bouillon kettle. Cover; bring to a boil. Lower heat and cook slowly until chicken is tender, 1½ to 2 hours. Remove chicken.

Strain broth through colander, mashing rice or barley through with liquid. Melt butter or chicken fat in soup kettle; blend flour smoothly with it. Stir strained soup into fat and flour mixture. Let cook 30 minutes, stirring frequently. Add 1 cup cream; stir and bring to a boil, but do not let boil. Beat yolks with remaining ¼ cup cream and stir into soup. Add salt and pepper if needed.

In each soup plate put a few even strips of breast of the boiled chicken. Pour hot soup over. Soup should be creamy, pale yellow, but not too thick. Serves 6.

GOOSE GIBLET SOUP À LA OFFENBACH

> *Goose heart, gizzard, wings, feet, and neck*
> *3 tablespoons butter*
> *2 small onions, sliced*
> *1½ quarts stock or bouillon*
> *1 small carrot, sliced thin*
> *1 small turnip, sliced thin*
> *3 tablespoons uncooked rice*
> *1 teaspoon salt*
> *Dash of pepper*
> *1 small tomato*
> *3 tablespoons heavy cream*
> *4 truffles, chopped fine*
> *1 teaspoon lemon juice*

Wash and drain goose parts. Slit gizzard and cut away tough section. Sauté all in soup kettle with butter and onions 5 minutes. Add stock or bouillon, vegetables, rice, and seasoning. Boil 30 minutes. Remove wings, feet, and neck with slotted spoon and discard. Wash, peel, and chop tomato; add to soup. Boil 5 minutes.

Mix cream, truffles, and lemon juice. Stir into soup and serve. Serves 4.

LIVER BISCUITS

> *Rich biscuit dough or puff pastry*
> *Melted butter*
> *Cooked chicken livers, chopped*

Roll dough ¼ inch thick; cut with small round cutter. Brush with butter; add 1 teaspoon livers. Cover with another round of dough; crimp edges together. Bake in hot oven (450° F.) until biscuits are light and browned, about 12 minutes. Serve with soup.

FRESH EEL SOUP

> *3-pound fresh eel, skinned and cleaned*
> *4 ounces dried mushrooms*
> *1 teaspoon salt*
> *1 pint sour cream*
> *¼ teaspoon freshly ground black pepper*
> *¼ teaspoon paprika*
> *2 teaspoons rye flour*
> *3 tablespoons chopped fresh dill*

Cut eel in 2-inch pieces. Wash mushrooms; drain; cover with cold water; let stand 24 hours. Drain water and pour it over eel; add additional cold water to cover, about 1½ quarts of liquid all together; add salt. Cover. Bring to a boil, then lower heat and cook slowly until eel is tender, 25 to 35 minutes. Add mushrooms and stir. Remove eel from soup.

Add sour cream slowly to soup, stirring steadily. Add pepper and paprika. Mix flour with a spoonful of hot soup and stir into the kettle. Stir until soup boils. Add eel; bring to a boil again. Serve with chopped dill sprinkled on top. Serves 6.

> *Two New York gourmets, Crosby Gaige and G. Selmer Fougner, both writers, both connoisseurs of the bottled sunshine from the Rhine Valley, often argued about the relative merits of our eels matelots, and eels vinaigrette. But they were in harmonious and rapturous agreement on our Fresh Eel Soup.*

A dish easily made at home when your fish market advertises a catch of eels.

FRESH EEL SOUP, BERLIN STYLE
AAL BERLINER

> *2-pound fresh eel, skinned and cleaned*
> *1 pint May Wine (see recipe)*
> *1 quart light beer*
> *2 slices pumpernickel, grated*
> *Sprig parsley*
> *1 bay leaf*
> *½ teaspoon thyme*
> *4 tablespoons butter*

Cut eel in small pieces. Place in a kettle with wine, beer, pumpernickel, and herbs. (May wine may be bought in some wine stores.) Bring slowly to a boil, then simmer gently until fish is done, 25 to 30 minutes. Remove eel to a deep soup tureen. Add butter to soup in kettle. Stir until steaming hot. Pour over eel. Serves 4.

We serve this with new boiled potatoes.

CLAM CHOWDER
MANHATTAN STYLE

> *2 to 3 dozen fresh clams*
> *½ cup boiling water*
> *2 or 3 stalks celery, diced*
> *3 medium-size onions, sliced*
> *4 green peppers, sliced thin*
> *4 slices salt pork, cubed*
> *⅔ cup flour*
> *3 pounds ripe tomatoes, peeled and chopped*
> *1 teaspoon minced thyme*
> *1 bay leaf, crumbled*

1 clove garlic, chopped
6 medium-size potatoes, peeled and cubed
2 quarts chicken broth
1 teaspoon salt
¼ teaspoon pepper
3 tablespoons minced parsley

Scrub clams; rinse and drain; put in large kettle with ½ cup boiling water. Cover kettle; set it over heat until the steam opens the clams. Remove clams from shells; save all broth; chop clams.

Sauté celery, onions, and peppers with salt pork until the fat is melted and browning; sprinkle flour over this and mix smoothly. Add the broth from the clam kettle, tomatoes, thyme, bay leaf, garlic, and potatoes. Add chicken broth; stir. Cover and let simmer until vegetables are thoroughly cooked, 30 to 45 minutes. Season; add clams and parsley; stir and serve. Makes 2 quarts. Serves 6 to 8.

LOBSTER BISQUE

1 onion, sliced
1 leek, chopped
1 carrot, sliced
1 stalk celery, chopped
½ teaspoon thyme
1 bay leaf
1 teaspoon salt
Meat 2 small boiled lobsters
½ cup cognac
2 cups white wine or hot water
1 cup cooked rice
2 tablespoons butter
3 tablespoons cream
2 egg yolks, beaten

Heat 2 tablespoons butter in 2-quart kettle. Add onion, leek, carrot, and celery and brown lightly 3 minutes. Add herbs, seasoning, and lobster meat. Stir lightly over heat 5 minutes. Add ¼ cup cognac and the wine or water. Cover. Cook over low heat 15 minutes. Remove lobster meat; put through grinder, using finest knife, and return to kettle. Add rice; mix. Cover and boil 5 minutes. Strain mixture, then cook over low heat about 45 minutes, until thickened like cream.

Remove from heat. Add butter, cream, egg yolks, and remaining cognac. Reheat, but do not boil. Serve at once. Serves 4 to 6.

COLD FRUIT SOUPS
KALTE SCHALE

> *1 pound peaches*
> *1 pound plums*
> *1 quart water*
> *1 quart red wine*
> *1 pound sugar*
> *1 2-inch piece stick cinnamon*
> *2 teaspoons powdered arrowroot*
> *1 cup heavy cream, whipped*

Wash fruit; cut in half; remove seeds. Cover with water and wine in an enameled kettle. Add sugar and cinnamon. Cook until fruit is soft. Put through sieve. Reheat. Mix a little cold fruit mixture with arrowroot, stir into rest of juice, and boil 1 or 2 minutes. Chill. Serve in large soup plates, garnish with whipped cream. Serves 6.

Variations: Other fruits such as apples, cherries, raspberries, grapes, rhubarb, and currants may be used. Vary amount of sugar as needed; use more or less arrowroot, as needed to make smooth soup.

3.

FISH AND SHELLFISH

A thousand things, all complimentary, are said about our fish specialties by Lüchow's patrons, but if someone asked me to sum up the reasons for their popularity, taking skilled cookery for granted, I would say, "It is because they are fresh."

Every pound of prime fish that comes into our kitchens is fresh, not frozen. Salmon arrives by air express from Gaspé, Canada. Brook trout is flown in ice from Colorado, while red snapper and pompano are whisked up from Florida in the same manner.

If the menu says "English sole," it means just that—the very special kind of sole that comes only from the coast of the English Channel and, like the others, arrives here by air.

Once a week I go to New Jersey and select the fresh-water eels to be smoked for our specialties. When we buy Nova Scotia salmon and sturgeon, only center cuts from young fish are chosen. At the Fulton Fish Market we pick out the fresh local fish, shad in season, and other favorites.

Every lobster shipment is checked when it arrives to make certain they are all alive. Crabs arrive kicking from Maryland. Shrimp, oysters, mussels, and other shellfish come to our kitchen fresh every day from the fishing beds.

FILLETS OF SEA BASS SAUTÉED WITH WHITE GRAPES

> *4 small (1½ pounds each) sea bass or*
> *4 pounds sea bass fillets*
> *1 teaspoon salt*
> *½ teaspoon pepper*
> *3 tablespoons butter*
> *1 cup fresh or canned seedless grapes*
> *Juice 1 lemon*

Wash, scale, and clean fish. Remove heads, tails, and skin. Cut fillets from bones. Season fillets with salt and pepper. Cook in 2 tablespoons butter until tender and delicately golden, about 5 to 8 minutes.

If fresh grapes are used, wash, drain, and peel them. Drain canned grapes. Sauté grapes in remaining butter with lemon juice 2 or 3 minutes, until hot and steaming. Pour over fish. Serves 4 or more.

BOILED LIVE CARP, HORSERADISH SAUCE

> *6-pound carp*
> *1½ teaspoons salt*
> *1 cup white wine*
> *2 cups water*
> *½ onion, minced*
> *¼ pound mushrooms, chopped*
> *¼ teaspoon pepper*
> *2 tablespoons chopped parsley*
> *3 tablespoons grated fresh horseradish*
> *1 cup sour cream or heavy sweet cream*

Our chef says, "Buy live carp." Have it cleaned and cut in serving-size pieces. Rinse; pat dry. Rub salt lightly on each piece. Place in saucepan. Add wine, water, onion, mushrooms, pepper, and parsley. Bring to a boil. Cover; lower heat and cook gently 20 minutes, or until fish flakes when tested with a fork. Drain. Place on warmed serving dish. Cook pan juices rapidly to reduce them. Pour over fish.

Mix horseradish and cream; serve with fish. Serves 6.

COLD GASPÉ SALMON
SALM VOM GASPE

> *At Lüchow's this delicacy is prepared with a whole fresh salmon especially imported from the Gaspé Peninsula.*

> *2- to 3-pound fresh Gaspé salmon*
> *1 bay leaf*
> *3 cloves*
> *4 tablespoons vinegar*
> *Juice 1 lemon*
> *4 peppercorns*
> *1½ teaspoons salt*
> *1½ tablespoons plain granulated gelatin ·*
> *2 egg whites*
> *Cooked peas, asparagus, or string beans*
> *Parsley*
> *Lemon, sliced*

Wash, scale, and clean salmon. Place in shallow pan. Add 3½ cups cold water, or enough to cover. Add bay leaf, cloves, vinegar, lemon juice, peppercorns, and salt. Bring to a boil, then lower heat and let simmer 15 minutes, or until fish is done. Carefully remove fish to a platter or mold.

To 3 cups of the hot stock in which the fish cooked, add the gelatin. Stir to dissolve. Beat egg whites lightly and stir into stock. Cook slowly just to boiling, then let stand in warm place (double boiler over hot water) 30 minutes, or until broth clears and thickens slightly. Strain through cheesecloth. Pour over fish. Chill. Decorate with chilled cooked vegetables, parsley, and lemon slices. Serves 4 to 6.

NOTE: This can be done with shad; a delicious and very satisfactory variation because the shad bones are dissolved by the marinade.

SMOKED SALMON IN COCOTTE
GERÄUCHERTER LACHS MIT TRÜFFELN

This may be served as a hot hors d'oeuvre or, when baked in a larger casserole, as a luncheon dish. French cooks line the cocotte or casserole with short-crust pastry. The Lüchow dish omits the pastry. It is one of the gourmet specialties of the huge menu card which has confronted the famous and the hungry in this Fourteenth Street restaurant for seventy years.

4 thin slices smoked salmon cut in 1-inch pieces
1 or 2 truffles, chopped
4 whole eggs and 2 yolks, beaten
1½ cups light cream
1½ cups milk
Dash of pepper
Dash of grated nutmeg

Divide pieces of salmon in 4 individual casseroles. Sprinkle with truffles.

Mix eggs, cream, milk, and seasonings and pour over salmon and truffles, almost filling casseroles. Set them carefully in a shallow pan containing a little hot water. Place in a moderate oven (325° F.) and bake 30 to 40 minutes. Serve hot. Serves 4.

PLANKED BONED SHAD

     4 fillets boned shad, about ½ pound each
     1 teaspoon salt
     ¼ teaspoon pepper
     Olive oil
     8 slices bacon
     4 tablespoons butter, melted and mixed with
     1 tablespoon lemon juice
     4 planks for individual service, or 1 large plank
     4 cups hot mashed potatoes
     4 hot broiled tomato halves
     2 or 3 cups hot cooked string beans
     16 hot cooked asparagus tips
     4 slices lemon

Season fillets with salt and pepper. Brush lightly with oil. Broil under moderate heat until golden on both sides, 15 to 20 minutes.

Broil bacon until crisp.

Warm planks and place a cooked fillet on each; pour a little of the mixed lemon butter over, then top with 2 pieces cooked bacon. Use pastry tube or spoon and make a border of hot mashed potatoes around the plank. Place broiled tomato, string beans, and asparagus tips attractively around the fish. Garnish with lemon slice. Serve at once. Or omit lemon, set plank under broiler heat until potatoes are delicately brown. Remove plank, add lemon, and serve. Serves 4.

STUFFED SHAD ROE

> 2 good-size shad roes
> 2 hard-cooked eggs, chopped fine
> ¼ teaspoon grated nutmeg
> 2 or 3 tablespoons Béchamel Sauce (see recipe)
> 1 tablespoon chives
> ½ teaspoon salt
> ⅛ teaspoon pepper
> 1 cup boiling broth or bouillon
> ¼ cup Velouté Sauce (see recipe)
> 2 tablespoons Hollandaise Sauce (see recipe)
> 2 tablespoons whipped cream

Rinse roes; pat dry. Place each on a square of waxed paper. Make a cut lengthwise in the roe to form a pocket for stuffing.

Mix the chopped eggs, nutmeg, Béchamel Sauce, chives, salt, and pepper. Stuff the roes with mixture. Fold the waxed paper over each; close tightly at both ends by turning it under twice. Place in boiling broth, cover, and boil 10 minutes. Remove roes from paper to a warmed serving dish. Cover with sauce made by mixing the Velouté, Hollandaise, and whipped cream. Place under broiler heat a few seconds until lightly brown. Serves 2.

With this you should sip Schloss Johannisberger Cabinet, the aristocrat of Rhine wines, from the estate of Prince Metternich.

FILLET OF SOLE À LA FRIESLAND

> *4 fillets sole*
> *1 shallot, chopped*
> *1 teaspoon salt*
> *¼ teaspoon white pepper*
> *¼ cup white wine*
> *¼ cup fish stock or bouillon*
> *2 tablespoons butter*
> *2 tablespoons flour*
> *1 egg yolk*
> *¼ cup cream*
> *¼ cup Lobster Butter*
> *Rich puff Pastry Crescents*

Place fish and shallot in saucepan; season with salt and pepper; add wine and stock or bouillon. Cook uncovered 10 to 12 minutes, or until fish is tender and liquid is reduced to about half the original amount. Remove fish to shallow baking dish and keep it warm. Beat butter and flour together; stir into pan liquid and cook until slightly thickened. Beat egg and cream together; stir into sauce. Heat a moment, but do not boil.

Spread Lobster Butter over fish; pour hot sauce over. Garnish with crisp Pastry Crescents and set under broiler 2 or 3 minutes. Serves 4.

LOBSTER BUTTER:
> *¼ cup butter*
> *1 teaspoon lobster paste (bought)*
> *¼ teaspoon onion juice*
> *¼ teaspoon lemon juice*

Let butter soften at room temperature. Beat other ingredients into it until smooth and evenly mixed. Makes about ¼ cup.

Pastry Crescents: See Pastry for Pies recipe. Roll pastry about ¼ inch thick. Cut with small fancy crescent cutter. Place crescents on baking sheet; brush lightly with butter. Bake in hot oven (450° F.) 11 to 15 minutes, until puffed and browned. Use as described.

ENGLISH SOLE, PROVENÇALE

4 small English sole
1 teaspoon salt
¼ teaspoon pepper
Juice 1 lemon
¼ cup flour
2 tablespoons olive oil
1 shallot, chopped
3 tablespoons butter
1 garlic clove, chopped fine
2 large tomatoes

Ask fish dealer to clean the sole for cooking whole. If you have to do it yourself, cut off head diagonally and trim end of tail. Turn back skin either at head or tail and strip it off with a sharp pull. Scrape surface of fish. Trim fins; clean inside. Rinse, drain, and pat dry.

Season with salt and pepper; sprinkle with lemon juice; dip lightly in flour. Heat olive oil in skillet and cook fish until golden brown on both sides and done, about 10 minutes. Remove to hot platter and keep hot.

Cook shallot, butter, and garlic 2 minutes. Skin tomatoes, chop, drain off juice, and add pulp to garlic mixture. Stir and cook 5 minutes. Pour over fish. Serves 4.

SHELLFISH

DEVILED CRABS

6 crab shells or ramekins
1½ cups fresh crab meat
5 tablespoons butter
1½ tablespoons flour
¾ cup cream
2 eggs, beaten
½ teaspoon salt
1½ teaspoons prepared mustard
½ teaspoon paprika
⅛ teaspoon cayenne

Wash crab shells. Flake crab meat; remove any cartilage. Melt 1 tablespoon butter in a saucepan. Add flour and cream; boil until thick. Remove from heat. Add eggs, salt, mustard, paprika, and cayenne. Stir. Add crab meat. Mix well. Pack into shells or ramekins. Melt remaining butter and pour over filled shells. Brown quickly under broiler or in hot oven (400° F.). Serves 6.

Leonard Lyons told this story about opera singer and baseball fan, Helen Traubel. Miss Traubel dined at Lüchow's one evening and ordered a large lobster. "How large?" the waiter asked. Miss Traubel indicated the lobsters being served at the next table and said: "The lobster I want eats those." So this recipe might be just right for her, with maybe a little left over for Lyons.

CURRY OF LOBSTER À L'INDIENNE

1 tablespoon minced onion
1 tablespoon minced carrot
1 stalk celery, minced fine
¼ teaspoon mace
¼ teaspoon thyme
1 bay leaf, crumbled
2 tablespoons minced parsley
2 tablespoons butter
2 bouillon cubes, moistened in
2 tablespoons hot water
1 tablespoon flour
1½ teaspoons curry powder
1 teaspoon paprika
1 cup lobster stock (water in which lobsters boiled)
¼ cup cream
Meat from 2 freshly boiled lobsters
3 cups hot boiled rice
Indian condiments

Cook onion, carrot, celery, herbs, and parsley in heated butter until onion is transparent and browning. Stir in bouillon cubes, then flour. Mix smoothly. Stir in curry powder and paprika. Add stock and continue cooking and stirring until boiling. Add cream; stir until thoroughly blended, but do not let cream boil. Remove from heat.

Cut lobster meat in generous pieces. Add to sauce.

Serve with hot boiled rice and Indian condiments such as Major Grey's chutney, grated fresh coconut, ground nuts, smoked dried fish (Bombay duck), grated green pepper, chopped onions and chives. Serves 4.

STUFFED LOBSTER À LA MITCHELL

As a result of my childhood training in Sweden and later with many famous chefs, I have what has been called a superb collection of gourmet dishes. This is one of my favorite lobster recipes.

2 gallons water
1 onion
1 carrot
1 stalk celery, sliced
½ pound dill
½ pound parsley, chopped
2 bay leaves
2 cloves
1 teaspoon caraway seeds
2 teaspoons salt
Few peppercorns
4 medium-sized live lobsters
½ cup olive oil
½ cup tarragon vinegar
1 teaspoon English mustard
½ pound cut chives
Juice of 2 lemons
1 teaspoon salt
¼ teaspoon freshly ground pepper
½ cup olive-oil mayonnaise
2 tablespoons fresh Beluga caviar
3 hard-boiled eggs, chopped fine

Add vegetables, spices, and seasoning to water. Bring to boil and add the live lobsters. Cook for about 20 minutes. Drain and cool. Cut lobsters in half lengthwise. Remove meat from body and claws. Dice the lobster meat. Rinse the shells.

Blend oil, vinegar, mustard, chives, lemon juice. Add salt and pepper. Pour over lobster meat. Put in refrigerator one hour. Fill shells; top with olive-oil mayonnaise. Decorate with caviar and chopped eggs. Serve with cucumber salad. Serves 4.

LOBSTER NEWBURGH

6 lobsters, about 2 pounds each
Boiling water
1 cup butter
1 teaspoon salt
1 teaspoon paprika
1 cup sherry
2½ cups heavy cream
½ cup light Cream Sauce (see recipe)
6 egg yolks, beaten
Extra sherry

Plunge lobsters into kettle of boiling water. Cover; cook until shells are bright red, 15 to 20 minutes. Let cool. Remove shells and cut meat in 1-inch pieces.

Sauté lobster pieces in skillet with butter. Season with salt and paprika. Add sherry and simmer slowly until wine is absorbed. Add 2 cups cream and the Cream Sauce; stir and let simmer about ½ minute. Beat egg yolks with remaining ½ cup cream and stir into pan. Pour into chafing dish and heat. Add 4 tablespoons sherry wine to sauce. Stir 1 minute and serve. Serves 6 to 8.

LOBSTER THERMIDOR

2 2-pound live lobsters
Boiling water
4 tablespoons butter
1 small onion or shallot, diced
6 mushroom caps, diced
½ teaspoon salt
¼ teaspoon paprika

¼ *cup sherry*
½ *cup heavy cream*
¼ *teaspoon English mustard*
½ *teaspoon Worcestershire sauce*
¼ *cup Cream Sauce (see recipe)*
1 egg yolk, beaten
2 tablespoons whipped cream

Plunge lobsters into boiling water and boil 20 minutes. Drain.
Cut off heads and claws. Cut lobster open lengthwise on under-
side. Reserve back half of shells. Remove meat from shell and
claws.

Cut meat in small pieces. Sauté in butter with onion or shallot
and mushrooms. Season with salt and paprika. Cook 6 minutes.
Add sherry and cream. Simmer until thickened and reduced. Mix
mustard and Worcestershire and stir into lobster. The mixture
should be very thick.

Fill shells. Beat egg yolk into Cream Sauce and spoon over
lobsters. Top with whipped cream. Brown under broiler until
golden. Serves 2.

OYSTERS CASINO À LA LÜCHOW

24 large oysters in the shell
1 cup butter
Small clove garlic
2 tablespoons minced chives
1 green pepper, minced fine
1 canned pimiento, minced fine
1 teaspoon salt
Dash of pepper
1 teaspoon Worcestershire sauce
Juice ½ lemon
8 slices bacon

Scrub oysters; open and remove from shells; drain. Return oysters to largest half of shells. Arrange in shallow baking pans.

Soften butter. Mash garlic and add. Add rest of ingredients except bacon and mix smoothly. Spread spoonful on each oyster. Cut each piece of bacon in 3 pieces and garnish each oyster with ⅓ slice. Set pan under moderate broiler heat until bacon cooks lightly. Then set pan in a hot oven (425° F.) 5 minutes. Serves 4 to 6.

CHICKEN FRIED SHRIMPS WITH TARTARE SAUCE

> *2 pounds fresh raw shrimps*
> *1 cup sifted flour*
> *1 tablespoon baking powder*
> *2 tablespoons sugar*
> *½ teaspoon salt*
> *2 eggs, beaten*
> *2 tablespoons melted butter*
> *1 cup milk*
> *Fat or oil for deep frying*
> *Tartare Sauce (see recipe)*

Wash shrimps; drain. To clean, clip shell with kitchen scissors, following black line. Remove shell, leaving last section and tail intact. Cut slit down center of back and remove black line (intestine). Rinse, drain, and dry thoroughly.

To make batter, sift dry ingredients; stir in eggs, butter, and milk. Beat lightly.

Dip shrimps in batter 1 at a time, holding by tail. Fry in deep hot fat (375° F.) until golden brown. Drain on thick paper toweling. Serve hot with Tartare Sauce. Serves 6.

NOTE: Use this same batter for fried chicken, oysters, fish.

4.

POULTRY AND GAME BIRDS

It takes a good part of the United States to supply
Lüchow's with ducks, chickens, and turkeys, because,
as everyone knows, the best fowl depend on the seasons as well
as the seasonings.

Consider the humble chicken, for example. The best of them
come from the farms about Schroon Lake in the Adirondacks.
They are wire-mesh-raised broilers, hens, and capons, and their
great virtue is a predominance of white meat, sweet and tender,
in their well-fleshed bodies.

No one disputes the pre-eminence of the ducklings raised on
the farms of Long Island. We buy ducks weighing about five and
a half pounds each when the weight is not due to excess fat at
the expense of meat.

Our guinea hens, no matter where their home may be, are
selected by the color of the meat. If it looks bluish, the hen is
usually tough.

Wisconsin produces the select geese we buy. They must be
stall-fed, a special process well known to the German-Scandi-
navian population which inhabits that rich state. The liver from
these geese, for which there is no substitute, is used for our
homemade pâté de foie gras.

We buy game birds from several different sections of the country, depending on which produces the best supply in a given season. Domestic partridge is better than the English variety and is much more in demand by American gourmets.

ROAST STUFFED PHILADELPHIA CAPON

> *1 plump 3- to 4-pound capon, cleaned and dressed*
> *Salt*
> *Heart, liver, gizzard*
> *1 cup bread crumbs*
> *¼ pound butter*
> *2 eggs, beaten*
> *1 tablespoon minced parsley*
> *Pepper to taste*
> *¼ teaspoon grated nutmeg*
> *1 tablespoon lemon juice*
> *½ cup chopped mushrooms*
> *3 truffles, chopped*
> *2 slices bacon*
> *½ tablespoon flour*
> *½ cup milk*
> *1 cup hot water*

Rinse capon inside and out and pat dry. Rub salt inside and out.

Chop heart, liver, and gizzard (remove tough membrane of gizzard). Mix with crumbs, 1 tablespoon butter, eggs, parsley, pepper, nutmeg, lemon juice, mushrooms, and truffles. Stuff capon; close opening with skewers or sew up.

Place stuffed capon in baking pan with bacon strips across breast. Dab with pieces of butter. Bake uncovered in moderate oven (375° F.) 25 minutes. Lower heat to 325° F. and continue roasting 45 minutes, or until capon is done.

Baste often with juices in pan and additional melted butter.

Add a little hot water to fat in pan so it does not get too brown. When chicken is done, remove to warmed platter.

To make gravy, stir flour into fat in roasting pan. Add milk, stirring smoothly. Stir in hot water gradually. Let boil until smooth. Serve with capon. Serves 4 to 6.

BREAST OF CAPON, MAI ROSE

> 2 *small slices Virginia ham*
> 2 *capon breasts*
> ½ *teaspoon salt*
> *Dash of pepper*
> 3 *tablespoons flour*
> 1 *teaspoon chopped shallots*
> 3 *fresh mushroom caps*
> ⅓ *cup May Wine (see recipe)*
> ½ *cup light cream*
> 1 *egg yolk, beaten*
> 1 *ripe tomato, peeled*

Cook ham in a hot skillet until tender and golden. Remove ham and keep it warm. Rinse chicken; pat dry. Season with salt and pepper. Dip lightly in flour. Sauté in ham fat until golden and tender, about 40 minutes.

Place ham on warmed serving dishes. Arrange breast of chicken on each piece.

Add shallots, mushrooms, and 1 teaspoon flour to the frying pan. Stir and brown lightly. Add May Wine and cream, alternately. Stir slowly after each addition. Add beaten yolk. Squeeze juice from tomato; chop and add. Stir and cook 1 minute. Pour over chicken and ham and serve. Serves 2.

CHICKEN FRICASSEE, BERLINER ART

*This elaborate and delicious chicken fricassee, in the
style of luxurious home dining of Berlin pre-war days,
is one of our specialties.*

2 2½-pound chickens, cleaned and disjointed
4 tablespoons butter
4 peppercorns
¼ teaspoon thyme
2 or 3 bay leaves
1 leek, sliced fine
1 small onion, sliced thin
1 carrot, sliced thin
1½ teaspoons salt
1 cup dry white wine
2 cups soup stock or bouillon
1 pint heavy cream
1 teaspoon flour
6 or 8 small pieces cooked lobster (lobster claw, says
   the chef)
½ cup chopped cooked tripe
½ cup sliced cooked mushrooms
4 to 6 cups hot cooked rice

Rinse chickens; drain. Remove bones. Melt butter in heavy iron
pot or Dutch oven and sauté chickens. Add peppercorns, thyme,
bay leaves, leek, onion, carrot, and salt. Cook chicken until
golden but not browned. Add wine and stock. Cover pan. Bring
to a boil, then cook over lowered heat 20 minutes, or until
tender.

Remove chicken to a warm serving dish. Stir cream into pan
and cook gently. Mix flour with a little of the hot gravy, then
stir it into kettle, cooking and stirring until mixture is the con-

sistency of a fricassee or smooth gravy. Strain sauce. Add lobster, tripe, and mushrooms. Reheat a moment and pour over chicken. Serve with hot rice. Serves 6 or more.

POACHED CHICKEN, KÖNIG'S GROTTE

> *2 medium-size (2½- to 3-pound) chickens, disjointed*
> *4 tablespoons butter*
> *1 stalk celery, chopped*
> *1 small onion, sliced*
> *1 carrot, sliced thin*
> *1 bay leaf*
> *¼ teaspoon thyme*
> *1 cup dry white wine*
> *1 pint light cream*
> *2 cups stock or chicken bouillon*
> *2 or 3 tablespoons flour*
> *1 teaspoon salt*
> *Dash of pepper*
> *Garnishes: sliced raw carrot, chopped green pepper,*
> *aspic cubes*

Rinse chickens; pat dry. Sauté in butter until lightly browned, 20 to 25 minutes. Place in kettle with celery, onion, carrot, bay leaf, and thyme. Pour wine, cream, and stock over all. Cover, bring to a boil, then lower heat and simmer 20 minutes, or until meat is thoroughly done.

Remove chicken. Cut meat from bones and place in four individual serving dishes.

Mix flour smoothly with a few tablespoons of the broth in which the chicken cooked, then stir the mixture into the remaining broth. Cook and stir until thickened to the consistency of a fricassee or cream gravy. Season. Strain this gravy over chicken. Let cool. When cold, garnish with sliced raw carrot, chopped pepper, and aspic cubes. Serves 4.

FRIED CHICKEN À LA VIENNOISE

> *2½- to 3-pound young chicken, disjointed*
> *1 teaspoon salt*
> *¼ teaspoon pepper*
> *½ teaspoon paprika*
> *¾ cup flour*
> *1 egg, beaten with*
> *2 tablespoons water*
> *1 cup fine cracker crumbs*
> *6 tablespoons butter*

Rinse chicken; pat dry. Season with salt, pepper, and paprika.
Roll each piece lightly in flour, then dip in the egg and water
mixture and roll in cracker crumbs. Sauté in butter very slowly,
about 35 minutes, or until golden on all sides and tender. Serve
with browned butter from the skillet. Serves 2 to 4.

CHICKEN PAPRIKA
PAPRIKA HUHN

> *2 young chickens, about 2½ pounds each*
> *½ tablespoon salt*
> *¼ pound butter*
> *1 large onion, diced*
> *2 teaspoons paprika*
> *½ tablespoon flour*
> *2 cups stock or bouillon*
> *1 tablespoon heavy cream*
> *1 cup thick sour cream*
> *2 tablespoons chopped fresh dill*

Rinse chickens; pat dry. Cut in serving pieces; season with salt.
Place in covered bowl in refrigerator 30 minutes.

Heat butter in deep pot or Dutch oven until light brown. Add onion and cook until transparent; stir in paprika. Add chicken. Cook slowly until pieces are golden, then cover and cook 30 minutes longer, or until tender. Sprinkle with flour. Add stock or bouillon and heavy cream; stir. Cover and let boil 15 minutes. Remove chicken to warmed serving dish. Stir sour cream into pot; stir and boil 5 minutes. Pour over chicken. Sprinkle with dill. Serves 4 to 6.

WHOLE CHICKEN IN CASSEROLE WITH VEGETABLES AND NOODLES
HUHN IM TOPF, GEMÜSE, NUDELN

> *2½-pound chicken, cleaned and drawn*
> *Chicken feet*
> *2 extra chicken wings*
> *2 extra chicken necks*
> *4 carrots*
> *4 small turnips*
> *2 leeks*
> *2 stalks celery*
> *1 teaspoon salt*
> *Few grains pepper*
> *1 bay leaf*
> *½ pound noodles*
> *Marrow Balls (or Dumplings)*

Rinse chicken, chicken feet, wings, and necks; drain. Put in large pot; cover with water.

Wash vegetables; scrape carrots; peel turnips and cut in quarters. Cut leeks and celery in 1-inch lengths. Add vegetables to pot. Add salt, pepper, and bay leaf. Cover. Bring to a boil, then lower heat a little and cook 30 to 45 minutes. Remove chicken and vegetables to a casserole; keep hot.

Strain broth. Cook noodles in broth; drain. Save broth. Add

noodles to casserole and keep hot. Cook Marrow Balls in remaining broth. Place on chicken and noodles. Serves 4.

MARROW BALLS (OR DUMPLINGS):

> *4 tablespoons fresh marrow, strained through sieve*
> *2 tablespoons butter*
> *3 eggs, beaten*
> *½ teaspoon salt*
> *Dash of pepper*
> *¼ teaspoon grated nutmeg*
> *2 tablespoons minced parsley*
> *1 cup fine cracker crumbs*
> *½ teaspoon baking powder*

Combine all ingredients and beat until smooth, using enough cracker crumbs to hold the mixture together. Form small marble-size balls. Cook in boiling broth 10 to 15 minutes. Lift out on slotted spoon. Serves 4 or more.

CHAFING DISH OF CHICKEN A LA KING

> *3½- to 4-pound fowl, boiled, or*
> *2 large chicken breasts, boiled*
> *4 mushroom caps*
> *1 green pepper*
> *2 tablespoons butter*
> *½ cup sherry*
> *2½ cups light cream*
> *2 egg yolks*
> *½ tablespoon diced pimiento*
> *½ teaspoon salt*
> *4 slices buttered toast*

Cut chicken meat in small pieces. Dice mushrooms and green pepper and cook in butter in chafing dish until pepper is tender. Add ¼ cup sherry; stir and let boil. Add 2 cups cream; stir; let simmer 2 or 3 minutes, until cream thickens. Add chicken; bring to a boil and boil 1 or 2 minutes.

Mix remaining ½ cup cream with egg yolks. Add to mixture slowly, stirring gently. Add pimiento and seasoning. Just before serving, stir remaining sherry into mixture. Cut toast in halves, diagonally. Serve creamed chicken on toast. Serves 4.

CHICKEN PAPRIKA WITH EGG BARLEY

This is the favorite Lüchow dish of George Mac-Manus, whose cartoons have made the world a more amusing place.

First, our chef explains, "egg barley" is the name of a miniature noodle, a tiny fleck of a noodle, about the size of a grain of barley. If you can't find this type of noodle at your grocer's you can cut homemade noodles very fine and get something of the same effect in this delicious German-Austrian dish.

2 medium-size onions, chopped
4 slices bacon
2 2½-pound chickens, disjointed
1 teaspoon flour
1 clove garlic
1½ cups white wine
2 quarts chicken stock or bouillon
1 teaspoon paprika
½ cup sour cream
2 cups egg barley or finely chopped noodles
2 tablespoons chicken fat
1 bay leaf

Cook 1 onion and bacon together 2 or 3 minutes in heavy kettle or Dutch oven. Add chicken and sauté until golden brown on all sides, about 25 minutes. Remove chicken.

Stir flour into fat remaining in pan. Add garlic, stir, and cook

1 or 2 minutes. Add wine, 1 quart chicken stock, and seasoning. Put chicken in this mixture. Cover and let cook gently 20 minutes, or until chicken is done. Add sour cream; stir. Serve with egg barley. Serves 6 or more.

TO PREPARE EGG BARLEY:

Place egg barley or fine noodles in a baking pan. Add chicken fat, other onion, bay leaf, and remaining stock or broth. Bake in moderate oven (375° F.) 20 minutes. Serve with Chicken Paprika. Serves 6 to 8.

FRICASSEE OF CHICKEN GIBLETS WITH RICE

> *Giblets of 4 plump hens (buy only giblets)*
> *½ teaspoon salt*
> *Dash of pepper*
> *3 cups boiling water*
> *2 carrots*
> *1 leek*
> *4 small onions*
> *1 stalk celery*
> *2 tablespoons butter*
> *2 tablespoons flour*
> *2 cups stock from giblets*
> *1 cup white wine*
> *1 tablespoon lemon juice*
> *2 egg yolks, beaten*
> *½ cup thick cream*
> *1 cup rice, boiled*

Wash and drain giblets. Season with salt and pepper; cover with boiling water. Dice all vegetables and add. Bring to boil, then lower heat and cook until giblets are tender, 30 to 45 minutes. Strain. Discard vegetables.

Melt butter; stir flour smoothly into it. Add stock, stirring slowly. Gradually add wine. Stir and boil until slightly thickened.

Add lemon juice; mix. Add giblets and, when hot, stir in egg yolks mixed with cream. Heat to steaming. Pour over rice in casserole. Serves 4.

CHICKEN LIVERS SAUTÉED WITH APPLES AND ONION RINGS

> *12 chicken livers*
> *½ teaspoon salt*
> *¼ teaspoon paprika*
> *2 tablespoons flour*
> *3 tablespoons butter*
> *½ Spanish onion sliced in rings*
> *4 apple slices about ½ inch thick*
> *2 tablespoons sugar*

Rinse and drain livers. If very large, cut in half. Season lightly with salt and paprika. Sprinkle lightly with flour. Cook gently in 2 tablespoons butter until browned.

In another small pan cook onion in a little butter; sprinkle over cooked livers.

In a third pan brown apple slices in remaining butter. Sprinkle with sugar to give glaze and flavor. Top liver and onions. Serves 2.

> *A very popular dish at Lüchow's and a favorite of Henry Kaiser and Rosalind Russell.*

VIENNESE BAKED CHICKEN
WIENER BACKHENDL

> *3 young chickens (about 2½ pounds each), cleaned and drawn*
> *1 tablespoon salt*
> *1 cup flour*
> *3 eggs, beaten with*

¼ *cup water*
2½ cups fine bread crumbs
Fat for deep frying
1 lemon, sliced

Rinse chickens; drain. Cut each in half; pat dry. Sprinkle with salt. Roll each piece in flour. Dip in egg, then in crumbs.

Fry in deep hot fat, lowering each piece carefully into fat to avoid shaking crumbs off.

When golden brown, place in baking pan and bake in hot oven (400° F.) until well browned. Lower heat to 325° F. after crust is firm, and continue baking until done, about 40 minutes in all. Place on thick paper toweling in a pan; set in oven, but leave oven door open. Season lightly with salt. Garnish with lemon and serve on warmed platter. Serves 6.

HALF CHICKEN, HUNGARIAN STYLE
HUHN, UNGARISCHE ART

2 young chickens, about 2½ pounds each
½ tablespoon salt
¼ pound butter
1 large onion, diced
2 teaspoons Hungarian paprika
1 tablespoon flour
1 cup stock or bouillon
1 tablespoon heavy cream
3 cups hot boiled rice
2 tablespoons minced fresh dill

Rinse chickens; pat dry. Cut in halves. Season with salt. Place in covered bowl in refrigerator 30 minutes.

Heat butter in deep pot or Dutch oven until light brown. Cook onion until transparent; stir in paprika. Add chicken. Cook slowly until golden, then cover and continue cooking 45 minutes, or until tender. Sprinkle with flour. Add stock or bouillon and cream. Cover pot and let boil 15 minutes. Remove chicken to warmed serving dish. Garnish with mounds of hot rice. Cook sauce down and pour over chicken. Sprinkle with dill. Serves 4.

DUCKLING IN ASPIC
BERLINER ENTENWEISSAUER

> *6-pound duckling, cleaned and drawn*
> *2 teaspoons salt*
> *1 small onion*
> *2 or 3 small carrots*
> *1 or 2 pieces celery or celery leaves*
> *1 sprig parsley*
> *2 cloves*
> *4 peppercorns*
> *1 bay leaf*
> *2 cups dry white wine*
> *2 tablespoons vinegar*
> *1 or 2 pickles, sliced*
> *2 hard-cooked eggs, sliced*
> *1½ tablespoons plain granulated gelatin*
> *2 egg whites*

Rinse duckling inside and out. Season with salt. Place in pot with onion, carrots, celery or celery leaves, parsley, cloves, peppercorns, and bay leaf. Add wine and vinegar and enough water to cover the bird. Bring to a boil, then lower heat, cover, and cook slowly until bird is tender, about 20 minutes per pound. Test with fork after first 30 minutes.

When duckling is tender, remove and cut in 4 portions. Place on serving dish; garnish with sliced pickles, hard-cooked eggs, and sliced carrots from stewing kettle.

Strain stock from kettle. Measure, and add gelatin in the proportion of 1 tablespoon gelatin to 2 cups stock. Let gelatin soften.

Beat egg whites slightly; stir into gelatin and stock. Reheat to boiling; remove from heat. Let stand until clear and slightly thickened. Pour over duckling. Chill in refrigerator. Serves 4.

ROAST WATERTOWN GOOSE WITH STEWED APPLES
MAST GANS MIT ÄPFELN

> *Stall-fed fat young goose, 12 pounds*
> *Salt*
> *4 cups water*
> *½ onion, sliced*
> *6 peppercorns*
> *¼ pound butter*
> *2 tablespoons flour*
> *Stewed Apples*

Have goose cleaned and drawn, the wings, neck, head, and feet chopped off. Wash goose inside and out; drain. Cover with cold water and let soak 15 minutes. Drain; pat dry. Rub with salt inside and out.

Place in baking pan. Add water, onion, and peppercorns. Roast in moderate oven (325° F.). When water has boiled down, baste frequently with butter which has been browned. A young goose should be cooked 15–20 minutes per pound.

Remove goose to warmed platter. Place pan on top of range. Stir flour into fat. Add 2 cups water. Stir and let boil 2 or 3 minutes, until smooth and slightly thickened. Serve with goose. Serves 6.

STEWED APPLES:

> *2 pounds apples*
> *2 tablespoons butter*
> *½ cup sugar*
> *½ cup water*
> *½ cup white wine*

1 small piece lemon peel
1 tablespoon lemon juice

Wash apples; peel and core. Cut fruit in thick slices. Sauté in butter 2 or 3 minutes. Sprinkle with sugar. Add water, wine, lemon peel, and lemon juice. Cover; cook slowly until apples are tender. Serves 6.

GOOSE IN WINE ASPIC
GANS IN GELEE, HAMBURGER ART

> *8- to 10-pound young goose, cleaned and drawn*
> *Boiling water*
> *2 or 3 sprigs parsley*
> *1 bay leaf*
> *1 onion, chopped*
> *½ teaspoon thyme*
> *1 clove garlic, crushed*
> *Pinch of salt*
> *6 peppercorns*
> *2 cups chopped celery*
> *4 whole allspice*
> *3 cups dry white wine*
> *4 pickles, sliced*
> *4 hard-cooked eggs, sliced*
> *1 carrot, sliced thin*
> *4 tablespoons granulated gelatin*
> *2 egg whites*
> *Mayonnaise or French dressing*

Rinse goose inside and out; drain. Place in large pot. Add about 2 quarts boiling water, parsley, bay leaf, onion, thyme, garlic, salt, peppercorns, celery, allspice, and wine. Bring to a boil, then lower heat, cover, and cook slowly 2 to 2½ hours, or until bird is tender.

When done, remove goose from liquid. Cut in serving pieces and arrange in large mold. Garnish with pickles, hard-cooked eggs, and carrot.

Strain stock (there should be about 8 cups). Add gelatin and when softened reheat stock. Beat egg whites slightly and stir into stock. When at boiling point, remove from heat. Let stand until clear and slightly thickened. Pour over goose in the mold. Chill until firm. Serve with mayonnaise or French dressing. Serves 6.

MEDALLION OF GOOSE LIVER À LA LÜCHOW

1 goose liver
1 cup milk
¼ cup water
½ teaspoon salt
Dash of pepper
1 egg, beaten
2 tablespoons flour
2 tablespoons butter
1 tablespoon madeira
Fried Apples and Onions (see recipe)
Truffles

Carefully remove gall from liver. Rinse liver; drain. Combine milk and water; add to liver. Let stand covered in refrigerator 2 hours. Drain. Pat liver dry; season with salt and pepper. Dip in egg, then in flour. Sauté in hot butter and madeira about 5 minutes, or until golden; turn liver several times. Remove to a warmed serving dish.

Serve with Fried Apples and Onions. Garnish with Truffles. Serves 1.

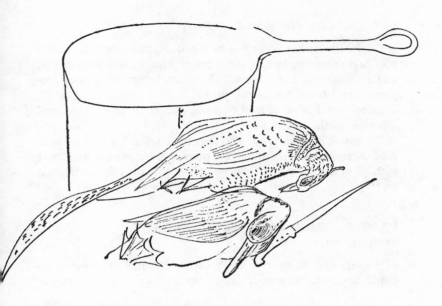

BREAST OF GUINEA HEN, SOUS CLOCHE

½ cup wild rice
2 tablespoons butter
½ small onion, chopped
½ cup chicken broth
Thin slice Virginia ham for 1 serving
Breast of guinea hen
¼ teaspoon salt
Dash of pepper
2 mushroom caps
Slice of toast
½ teaspoon flour
¼ cup sherry

Wash rice; drain; let dry. Sauté with onion in 1 tablespoon butter.
Add chicken broth; stir. Pour into small casserole. Cover and
place in moderate oven (325° F.), let simmer 45 minutes, or
until rice is tender and has absorbed liquid.

Cook ham in hot pan until browned. Remove ham and keep hot. Add remaining butter; sauté guinea breast. Add salt, pepper, and mushrooms. Cook about 15 minutes, turning guinea frequently and basting with pan juices.

In serving dish place ham on toast, guinea breast on ham, and top with mushroom caps.

To remaining pan sauce add flour; stir smoothly and let boil. Add sherry; stir. When steaming, pour over guinea breast. Cover with glass cloche or bell. Serve wild rice with this. Individual serving.

BABY PARTRIDGE WITH WINEKRAUT
REBHUHN IN WEINKRAUT

Prepare like Pheasant with Pineapple Kraut. Omit fresh pineapple; use 2 peeled, cored, and chopped apples in kraut mixture.

PHEASANT WITH PINEAPPLE KRAUT
FASAN MIT ANANAS KRAUT

> *2 young pheasants, cleaned and drawn*
> *1½ teaspoons salt*
> *Dash of pepper*
> *2 thin slices bacon*
> *2 tablespoons butter*
> *1½ pounds sauerkraut*
> *½ cup white wine*
> *1 cup diced fresh pineapple*
> *1 tablespoon flour*

Rinse birds. (Heads and feet should be removed.) Season lightly inside and out with salt and pepper. Place bacon slice on breast of each bird; tie in place or skewer with toothpicks. Sauté birds in butter 15 minutes, or until lightly browned. Place in deep pot, Dutch oven, or casserole.

Drain sauerkraut a little. Mix with wine and pineapple and surround birds. Cover and cook slowly 1 hour. When birds are done, remove from sauerkraut; remove skewer or toothpicks. Place birds on warmed serving dish. Stir flour into sauerkraut; cook a few minutes. Serve with birds. Serves 2 to 4.

> *Whenever pheasant is in season, Ed and Pegeen Fitzgerald choose this dish.*

LEFTOVERS

If you have small amounts of leftover cooked goose, duck, chicken, or other poultry, cut the pieces in narrow strips. Arrange in individual molds with sliced cooked vegetables, such as carrots and beets, and raw green peppers. Cover with stock aspic (as in Goose in Wine Aspic). Chill. Unmold on lettuce; garnish with sliced tomatoes and cooked green vegetables. Serve with mayonnaise or French dressing.

5.

MEATS AND GAME

A buyer who purchases supplies for a fine restaurant knows that the first consideration is to buy food of the best quality available. It is important in everything, large or small, but particularly in meats, which are the core of any restaurant's buying.

At Lüchow's we must make certain that the loins, ribs, and other beef products are of prime quality and proper age. Three and a half weeks is considered the right age for beef. Then it has begun to get tender without acquiring a gamy flavor.

To make the schnitzels and other Austrian dishes for which Lüchow's has always been famous, we require Detroit white veal from milk-fed baby calves. Lamb must be corn-fed spring lamb and no other. Pork comes to us from a supplier who has served us for thirty years and knows our specifications. He remembers that our pigs' knuckles must weigh one and a half pounds each. This is a cut slightly more than a knuckle and includes part of the shoulder, which is the tenderest part. When he sends us smoked pork loins, our man makes certain they are lean, because the lean retains more flavor than a fat portion when it is smoked.

The traditional German and Austrian game dishes on our menu are made with American-caught hare and venison. I find the fresh-killed Canadian hare best for many dishes, but it must be delivered to us packed in ice, not frozen. We prefer Wisconsin deer, because they are properly fed and the meat lends itself to aging, which is most important.

BEEF

BOILED BEEF, HANOVER STYLE

4 pounds beef plate
Boiling water
1 carrot, diced
1 small onion, diced
2 teaspoons salt
4 peppercorns
4 cloves
16 small boiled onions
2 pickles, sliced
2 hard-cooked eggs
1 7-ounce can tuna fish
1 egg yolk
2 cups olive oil
2 tablespoons capers
Caper vinegar
Stock from Boiled Beef

Wipe meat with damp cloth. Place in pot; cover with boiling water. Add carrot, onion, salt, peppercorns, and cloves. Bring to a boil, then lower heat, cover kettle, and simmer about 3 hours. Skim top occasionally.

When beef is done, remove it and slice. Garnish with cooked onions, pickles, and hard-cooked eggs. Pour over it a special sauce made as follows:

Flake the tuna fish and press through sieve. In a bowl beat egg yolk with olive oil, gradually adding fish to make a thick tuna mayonnaise. Add capers and a very little caper vinegar. To thin the sauce to gravy consistency, add a little stock from kettle in which the beef boiled. Serves 8 or more.

Boiled Beef is served with Between the Acts or Home Fried Potatoes.

Variations: Potatoes are diced, cooked in boiling beef stock (last 30 minutes) for Rinderbrust, Meerettig Sauce, Brühkartoffel.

When vegetables are omitted and noodles are cooked in the pot with the beef, the dish is called Rinderbrust mit Nudeln im Topf.

BOILED BEEF

4 pounds fresh beef (about 3 ribs)
1½ teaspoons salt
Boiling water
2 or 3 sprigs parsley
4 peppercorns
½ teaspoon thyme
2 onions, peeled
2 carrots, scraped
1 parsnip, peeled
1 small turnip, peeled
1 bay leaf
Horseradish Sauce (see recipe)

Wipe meat with damp cloth. Rub with salt. Place in pot. Cover with boiling water; bring to a boil quickly and boil 10 minutes. Skim top. Add parsley, peppercorns, and thyme. Cover pot, reduce heat, and cook slowly 2½ to 3 hours. For last hour of cooking add vegetables and bay leaf.

Remove vegetables when done and use them as garnish in

Boiled Beef Bürgerlich. Use the broth from the pot for soup. Serve Boiled Beef with Horseradish Sauce and plain boiled vegetables. Serves 2 to 4.

Boiled Beef with Sauerkraut (RINDERBRUST SAUERKRAUT):
Omit assorted vegetables; serve beef with sauerkraut.

> *The list of famous Lüchow patrons of the past and present who have feasted on the Boiled Beef reads like a World Who's Who. Caruso preferred this beef dish to all others in the restaurant. He often began his dinner with pigs' knuckles, then ate Boiled Beef, and with his dinner drank a dozen steins of beer. H. L. Mencken follows the same formula. It is also the favorite Lüchow dish of Ed and Pegeen Fitzgerald.*
>
> *Flo Ziegfeld was another Boiled Beef devotee. Herbert Bayard Swope and Irving Berlin order the Boiled Beef* mit *sauerkraut. So do Owen D. Young, Roy Howard and Walter P. Chrysler, Jr.*

BOILED BEEF IN CASSEROLE, BOURGEOISE
RINDERBRUST BÜRGERLICH

> *4 large serving-size pieces boiled beef*
> *2 cups Brown Sauce (see recipe)*
> *4 small boiled onions*
> *4 small boiled carrots*
> *2 tablespoons butter*
> *1 teaspoon salt*
> *1 teaspoon sugar*
> *8 Parisienne Potatoes (see recipe)*

Place meat in casserole; cover with Brown Sauce. Cook onions and carrots 3 or 4 minutes in hot butter; season with salt and sugar. Add to casserole. Cook in hot oven (400° F.) 25 minutes. Baste meat frequently with sauce. Add potatoes; continue cooking 10 minutes. Serves 4.

BOILED BEEF IN CASSEROLE, BÜRGERLICH

> *1 thick slice boiled beef*
> *1 hot boiled potato*
> *½ cup beef broth from pot in which beef boiled*
> *2 tablespoons cooked peas or lima beans*
> *1 small sour gherkin*
> *1 tablespoon Sauerbraten gravy (see Sauerbraten
>   recipe)*

Place slice of boiled beef in small casserole. Add potato, a little beef broth, small amount of cooked green vegetable, or wine kraut, the gherkin, and sauerbraten gravy. Set under moderate broiler. Heat 5 to 6 minutes to heat through. Serve in casserole. Individual serving.

BEEF À LA MODE
GEDÄMPFTE RINDERBRUST

> *6 pounds fresh brisket of beef*
> *1 tablespoon salt*
> *Dash of pepper*
> *1 quart red wine*
> *2 tablespoons beef suet or butter*
> *Flour*
> *1 calf's foot or veal bone*
> *1 cup chopped, drained tomatoes*
> *1 clove garlic*
> *2 sprigs parsley*
> *1 bay leaf*
> *1 quart stock or bouillon*
> *6 small carrots*
> *12 small onions*
> *1 tablespoon butter*

Season beef with salt and pepper. Pour wine over meat; let stand in covered crock 2 or 3 hours in the refrigerator. Turn beef several times during this period. When ready to cook, remove meat from marinade; pat dry. Brown in hot fat in deep iron kettle or Dutch oven. Sprinkle flour in bottom of pot; mix and stir with fat. Add calf's foot or bone, wine marinade, tomatoes, garlic, herbs, and enough stock barely to cover meat. Bring to boil. Lower heat, cover pan, and cook slowly about 2 hours.

Boil carrots. Sauté onions in a little butter until delicately browned. Remove meat from pot. Strain gravy. Return meat to pot; add carrots, onions, and gravy. Bring to boil and cook 30 minutes to 1 hour longer. Test for doneness. Serves 6.

Potato Pancakes are always served with the Rinderbrust.

BOILED BEEF HASH OMELET
HOPPEL-POPPEL, KOPFSALAT

> *2 cups diced boiled beef*
> *1 onion, chopped*
> *1 or 2 slices bacon, chopped*
> *2 tablespoons butter*
> *2 eggs, beaten*
> *Salt and pepper, if needed*

Cook beef, onion, and bacon in butter until hot and bacon is cooked. Add eggs and spread in pan; season; let bottom brown like omelet. Fold over and serve. Serves 2 or 3.

Serve with hearts of lettuce salad.

HASH, À LA LÜBECK

> *Rich pie pastry for 1-quart casserole or pie dish*
> *3½ cups chopped cold roast beef*
> *2 teaspoons chopped capers*

    4 anchovies
    3 eggs, beaten
    3 tablespoons bread crumbs
    ¼ teaspoon pepper
    ¼ teaspoon grated nutmeg
    1 teaspoon salt
    Caper Sauce (see recipe) or
    Anchovy Cream Sauce (see recipe)

Line casserole with pie pastry. Mix beef with other ingredients. Add 1 more beaten egg if necessary for smooth, slightly moist mixture. Pour in casserole. Cover top with pie pastry; crimp top and bottom pastry together in a decorative edge; gash top in simple leaf pattern. Bake in moderate oven (350° F.) 45 minutes to 1 hour, or until crust is golden. Serve with Caper Sauce or Anchovy Cream Sauce. Serves 6.

GERMAN BEEF RAGOUT
RAGOUT À LA DEUTSCH

    3 pounds bottom round of beef
    1 pound onions, diced
    1 or 2 tablespoons beef fat or shortening
    1 veal kidney
    1 teaspoon salt
    Dash of pepper
    ½ teaspoon paprika
    1 tablespoon flour
    3 cups stock or hot water
    1 cup tomato purée or chopped tomatoes
    1 bay leaf
    1 teaspoon chopped caraway seeds
    4 carrots, scraped and diced
    4 small turnips, peeled and diced
    4 medium-size potatoes, peeled and diced

Wipe meat with damp cloth. Dice beef and sauté with onions in fat until onions are transparent.

Rinse kidney; cut off any excess fat. Slice kidney into pan with beef and onions. Season with salt, pepper, and paprika. Cover and let cook slowly 30 minutes. Stir frequently. Add flour; stir and mix well. Add stock or water to cover meat mixture well. Add tomato purée or tomatoes. Mix and bring to boil, then lower heat and cook slowly 30 minutes. Add bay leaf, caraway seeds, and vegetables. Cover and let simmer 1 hour. Serves 6 or more.

Tyrolienne Alps Ragout: Omit veal kidney from above recipe.

BRESLAUER STEAK, CASSEROLE

3 pounds porterhouse steak, 1 inch thick
1 slice fat salt pork
2 cups Brown Sauce (see recipe)
6 small boiled onions
6 small boiled white turnips
4 tablespoons butter
2 teaspoons sugar
1 teaspoon salt
12 Parisienne Potatoes (see recipe)

Pound steak well. Cut salt pork in small pieces and heat in frying pan. Brown meat in the fat, cooking until lightly browned on all sides.

Place meat in casserole. Pour Brown Sauce over it. Cover; bake in slow oven (250° F.) until tender, about 2½ hours. Turn steak after first hour of cooking; baste frequently with sauce in casserole.

Brown onions and turnips in butter; season with sugar and salt. Add to casserole with Parisienne Potatoes. Serves 6.

LÜCHOW HAMBURGER

3 pounds beef
½ pound veal kidney fat or beef suet
4 or 5 slices white bread soaked in a little water
1½ teaspoons salt
½ teaspoon pepper
¼ teaspoon grated nutmeg
2 eggs, beaten

Mix meat and fat. Squeeze as much water as possible from bread. Add bread to the meat; mix smoothly. Add seasonings and eggs. Combine well. Shape in large patties. Broil or cook in a little fat in a hot pan until browned and done as desired. Serves 8.

When Fritz Kreisler dines here the Lüchow Hamburger is one of his favorite dishes. For their dessert, Mr. and Mrs. Kreisler enjoy one of the great German Pancakes.

Frank Sullivan, whose humor has delighted thousands of magazine readers for many years, is another Lüchow Hamburger enthusiast. And so are Dorothy and Lillian Gish, Eddie Cantor, Linda Darnell, Helen Hayes, and H. L. Mencken.

BROILED DEVILED SHORT RIBS

3 pounds short ribs of beef
Salt and pepper
4 teaspoons English mustard
¼ cup olive oil
¼ cup bread crumbs
Mustard Sauce (see recipe)

Wipe meat with damp cloth. Season with salt and pepper. Place in roasting pan and roast in moderate oven (325° F.) until tender, about 27 minutes per pound. Baste frequently with juices in pan.

Let cool. Cut in serving pieces, each piece containing a bone. Spread with mustard and oil. Cover with crumbs. Broil under moderate heat until browned. Serve with Mustard Sauce. Serves 4.

VIENNA STEAK AND POTATOES
WIENER ROSTBRATEN

> *4 ½-pound Delmonico (or club or sirloin) steaks*
> *1 teaspoon salt*
> *½ teaspoon pepper*
> *4 large onions, sliced*
> *3 tablespoons butter*
> *4 medium-size Idaho potatoes*
> *Fat for deep frying*
> *Few stalks watercress*
> *Small piece fresh horseradish root*

Wipe meat with damp cloth. Pound steaks very thin; season with salt and pepper. Sauté onions in butter until transparent; remove onions. Place steaks in hot fat and cook over high heat until delicately browned on each side and rare inside, about 10 minutes in all.

Peel potatoes; cut crosswise in ½-inch slices. Fry in deep hot fat (370° F.) until golden, 15 minutes. Place steaks on hot platter; cover with cooked onions; surround with fried potatoes. Garnish with watercress and a few shavings of fresh horseradish. Serves 4.

> *This is the favorite dish of Helen Traubel, Cole Porter, Lord Beaverbrook, and Sarah Churchill.*

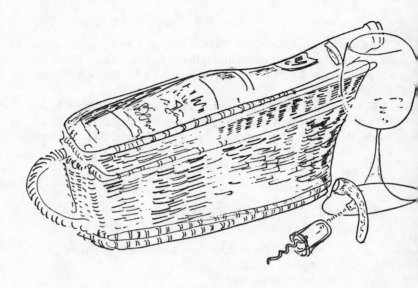

Walter Damrosch often lunched and dined at Lüchow's with his grandchildren. They ordered one of the following two dishes. The great conductor's favorite beverage always was a German red wine, Assmanshauser.

LÜCHOW'S BEEF STEAK TARTAR

> *2 pounds fillet of beef*
> *4 slices freshly buttered toast*
> *4 fresh raw eggs*
> *8 sardellen*
> *2 tablespoons capers*

Remove all fat from beef. Grind meat fine. Arrange on toast; serve raw egg on top of each slice. Garnish with sardellen and capers. Serves 4.

NOTE: If you are dieting to lose weight, this is a satisfying and effective dish.

RAW MEAT LUCULLUS
SCHLEMMERSCHNITTE

> *2 pounds fillet of beef*
> *4 slices freshly buttered toast*
> *4 tablespoons fresh black caviar*
> *1½ tablespoons chopped onion*

Remove all fat from beef. Grind meat fine. Arrange on toast; garnish with caviar; serve with chopped onions on a side dish. Serves 4.

NOTE: See diet note above.

> *This dish was a favorite of the great Pavlova and of John Barrymore, and still is of many show people.*

SLICED BEEF IN BROWN SAUCE

> *2 pounds beef*
> *1 teaspoon salt*
> *½ teaspoon pepper*
> *6 slices bacon*
> *2 tablespoons beef suet or butter*
> *4 mushroom caps, sliced*
> *2 tablespoons flour*
> *4 slices toast*
> *1 or 2 truffles, diced*
> *1 cup hot Brown Sauce (see recipe)*

The best beef for this dish is from the round. Wipe meat with damp cloth. Cut in slices about ¼ inch thick and 2 inches wide. Pound well. Sprinkle with salt and pepper. Lay bacon slice on each piece.

Sauté in hot fat with mushrooms. Sprinkle flour over. Cover pan and cook until bacon is done and meat tender, about 25 minutes. Place meat on toast; keep hot.

Add truffles to Brown Sauce; spoon over meat. Serves 4.

Serve with Braised Celery and Parisienne Potatoes.

POT ROAST WITH POTATO DUMPLING
SAUERBRATEN MIT KARTOFFEL KLÖSSE

> *3 pounds round steak*
> *1 tablespoon salt*
> *½ teaspoon pepper*
> *2 onions, sliced*
> *1 carrot, sliced*
> *1 stalk celery, chopped*
> *4 cloves*
> *4 peppercorns*
> *1 pint red wine vinegar*
> *2 bay leaves*
> *2 tablespoons kidney fat*
> *6 tablespoons butter*
> *5 tablespoons flour*
> *1 tablespoon sugar*
> *8 or 10 gingersnaps, crushed*
> *Potato or Bread Dumplings (see recipe)*

Wipe steak with damp cloth; season with salt and pepper. Place in earthen, glass, or enamelware bowl. Combine onions, carrot, celery, cloves, peppercorns, vinegar, and bay leaves and 2½ pints water, or enough to cover meat. Cover and put in refrigerator 4 days.

On fifth day remove from refrigerator, drain meat, sauté in kidney fat and 1 tablespoon butter in enamelware, glass or earthenware utensil, until seared on all sides. Add marinade liquid and bring to boil, then lower heat and let simmer about 3 hours.

Melt remaining 5 tablespoons butter in a pan. Stir flour smoothly into it. Add sugar, blend, and let brown to nice dark color. Add to simmering meat mixture. Cover and continue cooking until meat is tender, about 1 hour longer.

Remove meat to a warmed serving platter. Stir crushed gingersnaps into the pot juices and cook until thickened. Pour this special sauerbraten gravy over meat. Serves 6 or more.

Serve with Potato or Bread Dumplings. A fine full-bodied red wine is a fitting complement to this well-known dish. A favorite with our guests is Pommard Burgundy.

COLD SAUERBRATEN À LA MODE IN ASPIC

Leftover Sauerbraten makes a delicious dish in madeira-flavored aspic. Place a piece of Sauerbraten in a serving dish or mold. Cover and surround with aspic; decorate with fancy-cut raw and cooked vegetables; chill and serve.

MADEIRA ASPIC

3 cups beef broth or stock
1 cup madeira wine
2 tablespoons granulated gelatin

Heat most of broth or stock to boiling. Moisten gelatin with a little cold stock or water and stir into broth. Add any remaining stock and wine. Let stand until cool and slightly thickened. Pour over meat as described. Chill in refrigerator until firm. Makes 1 quart aspic. Serves 6 or more.

ROAST PRIME RIBS OF BEEF

At Lüchow's the standing rib roast weighs about 35 pounds. When this great piece of superb beef is half done, the chef adds whole onions, carrots, and spices to the pan to flavor the meat à la Lüchow. Here is his recipe for a family-size cut.

2- or 3-rib standing roast (4 to 5 pounds)
Salt
Pepper
2 small onions
4 carrots, quartered
2 tablespoons mixed whole spices

Wipe meat with damp cloth. Place, fat side up, in roasting pan. Mix 1 tablespoon salt and pepper (⅔ salt, ⅓ pepper) and rub this well into meat. Place in moderate oven (350° F.) to start. Do not cover. Do not add water. Baste frequently with drippings in the pan. When roast is half done, lower heat to 275° F. or 250° F. At this point add onions, carrots, and spices to pan. Continue basting meat frequently with pan juices.

For rare roast, allow 18 to 20 minutes per pound roasting time; for medium, 22 to 25 minutes per pound; for well done, 27 to 30 minutes per pound. Serves 8 or more.

Fred Allen, who has told his diet problems to a radio-listening world, often drools over the dishes named on our big menu but usually settles for roast beef, as that is his favorite.

SWEDISH MEAT BALLS

1 pound beef
1 pound pork loin
1 pound veal
2 tablespoons chopped shallots
2 cloves garlic, mashed
1 tablespoon chopped fresh dill
1 cup cream, whipped
2 eggs, beaten
½ cup sugar
Salt
Pepper
⅛ teaspoon cayenne
1 teaspoon Worcestershire sauce
4 tablespoons butter
Extra cream

Grind together beef, pork, and veal very fine, twice. Mix meat with shallots, garlic, dill, whipped cream, eggs, and sugar. Add salt and pepper to taste, cayenne, and Worcestershire. Stir and mix thoroughly with a wooden spoon until well blended and smooth. If necessary, add a little more cream.

Make into small, neat balls about 1 inch in diameter. Sauté in butter very slowly over medium heat. Do not disturb them. When half cooked, about 20 minutes, set pan in moderate oven (350° F.). After another 20 to 25 minutes, add cream to make a thin gravy. Add some chopped dill to gravy. Serves 6 to 8.

Serve with baked red kidney beans and a side dish of lingonberries.

ROULADE OF BEEF, AUGUST LÜCHOW

> 2 pounds top round of beef
> ½ teaspoon salt
> ¼ teaspoon pepper
> 1 medium-size onion, chopped fine
> 1 shallot, minced
> 1 clove garlic, minced
> ¼ pound beef, ground fine
> ¼ pound veal, ground fine
> ¼ pound pork, ground fine
> 1 tablespoon chopped parsley
> 1 teaspoon chopped chives
> 2 slices bread soaked in milk
> ½ cup cream
> 6 thin slices fat salt pork
> ¼ cup flour
> 2 tablespoons beef fat, butter, or margarine
> 2 large onions, sliced thin
> 2 or 3 carrots, sliced thin
> ½ teaspoon powdered cloves
> ½ teaspoon thyme
> 1 bay leaf

2 tomatoes, peeled and chopped
1 cup burgundy wine
1 cup veal stock

Wipe top round with damp cloth. Cut beef in 6 slices about 2½ inches by 4 inches and ½ inch thick. Place on board and pound well to about ¼ inch thickness. Season with salt and pepper.

Combine onion, shallots, garlic, ground beef, veal, and pork, parsley, chives, bread, and cream. Mix well. Spoon generous amount of mixture onto each piece of beef. Roll, wrap with slice of salt pork, and tie or skewer with toothpicks. Sprinkle lightly with flour.

Grease deep heavy pot or Dutch oven with beef fat, butter, or margarine. Place roulades in this; cover with sliced onions and carrots. Add cloves, thyme, and bay leaf. Cover pot and cook over high heat 8 to 10 minutes to brown meat. Turn roulades to brown on all sides. Add tomatoes, wine, and stock. Cover pot with waxed paper rubbed with beef fat or butter and placed fat side down. Set pot in moderate oven (350° F.) and cook until rolls are done, 30 to 45 minutes.

Remove roulades to a warmed serving dish (remove skewers or string). Set pot on high heat and boil pot sauce rapidly to reduce it. Strain, reheat if necessary, and pour over roulades. Serves 6.

Serve with hot vegetables such as glazed onions, new peas, and Parisienne Potatoes.

LAMB

LAMB CHOPS CHAMPILLON

6 loin or rib lamb chops
2 tablespoons butter
1½ pounds potatoes

1 pound onions, sliced
1 bay leaf
1½ teaspoons salt
½ teaspoon pepper
1½ cups beef or chicken stock, or bouillon
2 tablespoons minced parsley
4 tablespoons bread crumbs

Sauté chops in butter. Cover pan and cook 5 to 10 minutes, or until meat is delicately browned on both sides.

Wash potatoes; peel and slice thin. Add to meat with onions, bay leaf, salt, pepper, and enough beef or chicken stock to cover. Cover pot and let cook until meat is tender, 25 to 30 minutes.

Remove chops to a casserole. Cover with potato and onion mixture from the pot; sprinkle with parsley and bread crumbs. Brown in hot oven (400° F.) or under moderate broiler heat until top is golden. Serves 6.

PORK

BROCHETTE OF PORK TENDERLOIN
WITH WILD RICE AND SOUR SAUCE

1½ pounds pork tenderloin
4 slices bacon
8 mushroom caps
6 tablespoons butter
6 tablespoons bread crumbs
Wild Rice with Raisins (see recipe)
Sour Cream Sauce (see recipe)

Cut pork in pieces suitable for individual skewers (1½-inch cubes). Cut each slice of bacon in 4 pieces. Sauté mushrooms in 2 tablespoons butter. Place all on 4 skewers, starting with mushroom cap, then alternating bacon and pork, using 4 pieces of each meat on each skewer, and ending with mushroom. Melt remaining butter and sprinkle over filled skewers; roll each in crumbs. Place on broiler pan under moderate heat. Cook until browned on all sides and done, about 15 minutes. Serve on mound of Wild Rice with Raisins. Serve Sour Cream Sauce with this. Serves 4.

NOTE: Instead of cooking this on skewers, cut meat in 4 long, narrow pieces and broil until lightly cooked. Lay bacon on top and sautéed mushroom caps on top of bacon; sprinkle with crumbs. Continue broiling until bacon is cooked and all is well browned. Serve with Wild Rice with Raisins and Sour Cream Sauce as described.

LOIN OF PORK IN ASPIC
SÜLZ KOTELETT

> *3 or 4 pounds loin of pork*
> *1½ teaspoons salt*
> *1 small onion*
> *2 or 3 small carrots*
> *1 or 2 pieces celery or celery leaves*
> *1 sprig parsley*
> *4 cloves*
> *4 peppercorns*
> *1 bay leaf*
> *2 cups dry white wine*
> *4 tablespoons vinegar*
> *1 or 2 pickles, sliced*
> *2 hard-cooked eggs, sliced*
> *3 tablespoons plain gelatin*
> *2 egg whites*

Wipe meat. Season with salt. Place in pot with onion, carrots, celery or celery leaves, parsley, cloves, peppercorns, and bay leaf. Add wine and vinegar and enough water to cover meat. Bring to a boil, then lower heat, cover, and cook slowly until meat is tender, about 1 to 1½ hours. Test with fork after first hour.

When meat is tender, remove from pot and cut in 4 portions. Place on serving dish. Garnish with pickles, eggs, and the carrots from the stewing kettle.

Strain stock; measure. Add gelatin in the proportion of 1 tablespoon gelatin to 2 cups stock. Let gelatin soften. Beat egg whites slightly; stir into gelatin and stock. Reheat to boiling; remove from heat. Let stand until clear and slightly thickened. Pour over meat. Chill in refrigerator. Serves 4 or more.

SMOKED LOIN OF PORK
WITH SAUERKRAUT AND GRAPES
KASSLER RIPPCHEN GLACE

> *8 pounds smoked loin of pork*
> *Boiling water*
> *1 bay leaf*
> *8 peppercorns*
> *6 whole allspice*
> *2 cups fruit juice or white wine*
> *1½ cups brown sugar*
> *1 cup seedless grapes*
> *4 cups sauerkraut*
> *Burgundy Sauce (see recipe)*

Wash and scrub loin. Place in kettle; add boiling water barely to cover, bay leaf, peppercorns, and spice. Simmer. Allow 15 minutes' simmering time per pound; if loin is small, allow 30 minutes per pound.

When done, let cool in water in which it cooked. Drain; strip off skin. Place in baking pan and bake in hot oven (425° F.). Baste with wine or fruit juice; dredge with sugar. Lower heat to moderate (350° F.) and let brown 25 minutes, until glazed and shiny.

Wash and peel grapes. Mix sauerkraut, grapes, and juices from the pan; arrange kraut mixture around meat; let cook 15 minutes. Serve pork loin with sauerkraut and Burgundy Sauce. Allow ¾ pound meat per serving.

BARBECUED SPARERIBS

> *2 whole pieces spareribs weighing 1½ pounds each,*
> *cracked through center*
> *2 medium-size onions, quartered*
> *1 teaspoon salt*
> *¼ teaspoon pepper*
> *1 bay leaf*
> *3 cloves*
> *½ teaspoon mixed spices*
> *⅛ teaspoon thyme*
> *2 carrots, sliced thin*
> *1 teaspoon English mustard*
> *1 clove garlic, mashed*
> *¼ cup vinegar*
> *¼ cup sugar*
> *3 cups chili sauce*
> *1 tablespoon A1 sauce*
> *1 tablespoon Worcestershire sauce*
> *Stock or bouillon*

Place spareribs and onions in baking pan; season with salt and pepper. Brown under broiler, turning to brown both sides.

Tie bay leaf, cloves, mixed spices, and thyme in a small piece of cheesecloth. Place in pan; add carrots. Mix mustard, garlic, vinegar, sugar, chili sauce, A1, and Worcestershire, and pour over ribs. Add stock or bouillon barely to cover. Bring to a boil, then set in moderate oven (350° F.) to cook slowly until well done, about 1½ hours in all.

Remove ribs to hot platter. Remove spice bag. Strain gravy and pour over ribs. Serving is ½ pound per person.

DEVILED PIGS' FEET

> *4 pigs' feet*
> *1 large onion*
> *1 clove garlic, cut*
> *1 lemon, sliced*
> *2 bay leaves*
> *4 peppercorns*
> *1 teaspoon salt*
> *8 whole cloves*
> *4 tablespoons English mustard*
> *¼ cup olive oil*
> *¼ cup bread crumbs*
> *Mustard Sauce (see recipe)*

Wash and split pigs' feet in halves. Place in kettle with onion, garlic, lemon, bay leaves, peppercorns, salt, and cloves. Cover with water. Boil slowly until tender, about 2½ hours. Drain. Let cool. Place in shallow pan; spread pigs' feet with mustard and oil. Cover with crumbs. Broil under moderate heat until golden brown. Serve with Mustard Sauce. Serves 4.

Sauerkraut and mashed potatoes are always served with Deviled Pigs' Feet.

PIGS' KNUCKLES
METHOD OF CORNING:

> *2 gallons water*
> *1 pound salt*
> *1 teaspoon saltpeter*

Marinate pigs' knuckles in this solution for 10 days.

METHOD OF COOKING:

Cover pigs' knuckles with fresh water, no salt. Add small onion, cut in half, few peppercorns, few bay leaves. Boil 2½ or 3 hours, until tender. Serve with Sauerkraut.

Pig's Knuckle in Burgundy: After pig's knuckle has been boiled until tender, remove from water. Arrange pig's knuckle in baking dish on Weinkraut (see recipe). Cover with burgundy and brown in oven.

VEAL

HAM AND VEAL PÂTÉ

> *Rich pastry for large 2-crust casserole pie*
> *2 slices cold boiled ham, ½ inch thick*
> *2 slices cold veal schnitzel, ½ inch thick*
> *4 tablespoons fresh pork lard*
> *2 shallots, minced*
> *2 tablespoons minced parsley*
> *½ cup minced fresh or canned mushrooms*
> *2 or 3 eggs*
> *1½ teaspoons salt*
> *½ teaspoon pepper*

Line a deep loaf pan or casserole with pie pastry. Cut ham and veal in small round pieces.

To trimmings of ham and veal add lard, shallots, parsley, and mushrooms. Grind together very fine. Beat eggs into meat mixture; season with salt and pepper. Arrange alternate layers of meat and the meat mixture to fill baking dish. Cover with pastry; crimp edge decoratively; gash top in several places in a decorative pattern. Bake in slow oven (300° F.) 1½ hours, or until crust is golden. Serve warm or cold. Serves 4.

We recommend a delicate white still wine with this savory dish. Liebfraumilch, Blue Nun, is the choice of the gourmets who order this pâté on Fourteenth Street.

VEAL CUTLETS WITH FRIED EGGS
SCHNITZEL HOLSTEIN

> *4 6-ounce veal cutlets*
> *1 teaspoon salt*
> *¼ teaspoon pepper*
> *Flour*
> *5 eggs*
> *1 cup bread crumbs*
> *6 tablespoons butter*
> *8 or 12 anchovy fillets*
> *8 thin slices pickled beet*
> *4 or 8 slices dill or sour pickle*
> *Home Fried Potatoes (see recipe)*

Wipe cutlets with damp cloth. Pound meat thin; season; dip each cutlet in flour. Beat 1 egg. Dip cutlets in this, then roll in bread crumbs. Cook in 4 tablespoons butter until golden brown on both sides.

Fry the remaining 4 eggs in 2 tablespoons butter.

Remove cutlets to a warmed serving dish. Place fried egg on each; garnish with anchovy fillets, sliced beet, and pickles. Serve with generous helping of Home Fried Potatoes. Serves 4.

You'll be extra happy with this dish if you do as Lüchow patrons do and sip a fine Moselle wine with the Schnitzel. Piesporter Goldtröpfchen Auslese, from the Kesselstatt domain in Germany, is recommended by our competent guardians of the wine list on Fourteenth Street.

"The cars that purr up to its antique doors today are

streamlined," said Bob Considine in his Collier's, December 1950, article on Lüchow's, "but if you stay inside the mellow place long enough you see or sense the well-fed ghosts of its bygone diners: Al Smith come to wave a sensitive and grateful nose over a sizzling schnitzel."

Not only a sizzling schnitzel would greet Al of the famous brown head covering, but he loved the fragrance and the good things which preceded and followed this famous dish, and the comradeship of his many friends who made Lüchow's their favorite eating place.

Schnitzel Holstein belongs in the tradition of those great days.

VEAL CUTLETS À LA LÜCHOW
SCHNITZEL À LA LÜCHOW

4 8-ounce veal cutlets
6 tablespoons butter
1 cup stock
6 eggs
1 tablespoon chopped chives
1 teaspoon salt
¼ teaspoon pepper
10 medium-size fresh mushrooms, sliced
16 stalks hot cooked fresh asparagus

Wipe cutlets with damp cloth; pound. Cook in 4 tablespoons butter until golden on both sides and cooked through. Remove cutlets to warmed serving dish and keep hot.

Stir stock into pan gravy and cook until smooth and slightly thickened.

Beat eggs; add chives, salt, and pepper. Sauté mushrooms in remaining butter 3 or 4 minutes. Add egg and chive mixture to mushrooms; cook over moderate heat, stirring like scrambled eggs. Pour this mixture over cutlets. Streak with a little hot gravy. Garnish platter with asparagus. Serves 4.

BREADED VEAL CUTLET
WIENER SCHNITZEL

> *4 6-ounce veal cutlets*
> *Flour*
> *3 tablespoons grated Parmesan cheese*
> *1 egg, beaten*
> *1 teaspoon minced parsley*
> *½ teaspoon salt*
> *¼ teaspoon pepper*
> *¼ teaspoon grated nutmeg*
> *½ cup milk*
> *6 tablespoons butter*
> *Juice ¾ lemon*
> *Parsley for garnish*

Wipe meat with damp cloth; pound very thin; dip lightly in flour. Mix cheese, 2 tablespoons flour, egg, parsley, salt, pepper, nutmeg, and milk. Beat smooth. Dip floured cutlets in this batter. Cook over low heat in 4 tablespoons butter until golden and tender.

Remove cutlets to warmed serving platter and keep them hot. Heat remaining butter until darkened; add lemon juice. Stir and pour over cutlets. Garnish with parsley. Serves 4.

VEAL CUTLET WITH MUSHROOMS
NATUR SCHNITZEL MIT IMPORTIERTEN STEINPILZEN

> *2 8-ounce cutlets*
> *½ teaspoon salt*

⅛ *teaspoon pepper*
5 *tablespoons butter*
½ *shallot, chopped fine*
No. 1 can imported Limousin mushrooms (Stein-
    pilzen)
½ *cup stock or bouillon*
1 *tablespoon minced chives*

Pound cutlets thin; season lightly. Cook in 3 tablespoons butter
until golden on both sides and done.

Cook shallot in remaining butter until transparent. Drain
mushrooms; slice; add to shallot. Cook 2 or 3 minutes.

Remove cutlets to a warmed serving platter or 2 individual
hot dishes. Add stock to sauce in veal pan; stir and cook 1 or 2
minutes. Cover cutlets with shallot and mushroom mixture; pour
gravy over all. Sprinkle with chopped chives. Serves 2.

This Schnitzel is served with freshly boiled or rissole potatoes.

FILLET OF VEAL WITH KIDNEY

8 *medallions of veal, 3 ounces each*
1 *teaspoon salt*
½ *teaspoon pepper*
8 *slices veal kidney*
8 *tablespoons butter*
8 *large mushroom caps*
½ *cup stock or bouillon*
½ *cup white wine*

Wipe veal with damp cloth; season. Sauté with kidney in 6 tablespoons butter until well done. Sauté mushroom caps in remaining
butter, being careful not to break mushrooms. Remove veal to a
warmed platter; place kidney slice on each piece of veal and top
with mushroom cap. Stir stock and wine into pan in which meat
cooked; cook rapidly to reduce and thicken; stir and pour over
meat. Serves 4.

Serve with hot boiled potatoes, asparagus tips, and string beans.

FILLET OF VEAL WITH KIDNEY EN CASSEROLE

> *1 veal kidney*
> *1 pound veal cutlet*
> *½ teaspoon salt*
> *⅛ teaspoon pepper*
> *4 mushroom caps, sliced*
> *3 tablespoons butter*
> *¼ cup sherry*
> *2 cups assorted hot cooked vegetables, such as peas and string beans, or small lima beans and carrots*

Wash kidney; leave fat on. Slice, cover with cold salted water, and let stand 30 minutes.

Slice veal in 2 cutlets; pound until ¼ inch thick; season.

Drain kidney. Sauté kidney, veal, and mushrooms in butter until meats are tender and golden. Remove veal and kidney to a small casserole. Add sherry to pan; stir and let boil. Pour over meat. Garnish with mounds of hot cooked vegetables. Serves 2.

VEAL KIDNEY ON TOAST

> *2 veal kidneys*
> *½ teaspoon salt*
> *⅛ teaspoon pepper*
> *2 tablespoons butter, melted*
> *½ small onion*
> *1 cup roast veal gravy, or*
> *½ cup Brown Sauce (see recipe)*
> *3 tablespoons chopped mushrooms*
> *1 tablespoon lemon juice*
> *½ teaspoon sugar*

> *¼ cup red wine or madeira*
> *2 large pieces toast*

Wash kidneys. If fat is very thick, trim off some. Cut kidneys open and insert skewer in each to hold them flat. Season with salt and pepper and brush with butter. Broil 8 to 10 minutes on each side under moderate broiler heat, about 5 inches from heat.

Heat onion with gravy or Brown Sauce. When steaming, add mushrooms, lemon juice, and sugar. Stir and cook gently 1 or 2 minutes. Heat wine.

Remove skewers from kidneys. Place 1 kidney on each piece of toast; dash with hot wine, then spoon hot Brown Sauce over. Serves 2.

VEAL STEAK WITH PAPRIKA SAUCE
PAPRIKA SCHNITZEL

> *2 pounds veal steak*
> *1 teaspoon salt*
> *¼ teaspoon pepper*
> *3 tablespoons butter*
> *1 cup hot Paprika Sauce (see recipe)*

Have steak cut ½ inch thick. Wipe with damp cloth. Pound thin. Season with salt and pepper. Sauté in hot butter slowly until golden and tender. Place on hot serving dish. Spoon hot Paprika Sauce over it. Serves 4.

VEAL CHOPS NATURE
NATUR SCHNITZEL

> *4 veal chops*
> *½ teaspoon salt*
> *¼ teaspoon pepper*
> *3 tablespoons butter*

Wipe chops with damp cloth; season. Brown in butter at high heat, about 15 minutes. Reduce heat; cook slowly until tender and done, another 5 to 8 minutes. Serves 4.

MEAT BALLS
WITH CAPER AND SARDELLEN SAUCE
KÖNIGSBERGER KLOPS

> *1½ pounds raw veal*
> *¼ pound fat pork*
> *3 tablespoons butter*
> *1½ hard rolls*
> *2 tablespoons grated onion*
> *½ teaspoon grated lemon peel*
> *3 eggs, beaten*
> *½ teaspoon pepper*
> *1 teaspoon salt*
> *1 tablespoon lemon juice*
> *1 teaspoon Worcestershire sauce*
> *Chopped parsley*
> *1½ quarts stock or bouillon*

Grind meats very fine; mix with 2 tablespoons butter. Moisten rolls with water; when soft, squeeze water out and mix bread with meat.

Cook onion in remaining butter until browned. Add to meat mixture with lemon peel, eggs, pepper, salt, lemon juice, Worcestershire, and parsley. Mix thoroughly. Shape in 12 balls.

Heat bouillon or stock to boiling; drop balls in and simmer, covered, 15 minutes. Remove from stock with slotted spoon to a warmed dish and make gravy.

GRAVY

> *4 or 5 tablespoons butter*
> *4 or 5 tablespoons flour*

1 or 2 small boneless sardines
2 tablespoons capers
2 tablespoons chopped parsley
½ cup buttered crumbs

Measure stock. For every 2 cups of stock, mix 2 tablespoons butter with 2 tablespoons flour. Stir into hot stock; cook and stir until smooth and boiling.

Mash sardines with 1 tablespoon butter. Stir into gravy with capers and parsley. Reheat meat balls in gravy. To serve, cover top with buttered crumbs. Serves 4 or more.

At Lüchow's, noodles are usually served with the Klops.

CALVES' BRAINS WITH SCRAMBLED EGGS
GEBACKENES KALBSHIRN MIT RÜHREI

2 calves' brains
2 tablespoons vinegar
1½ teaspoons salt
5 peppercorns
½ onion, sliced
1 small carrot
2 sprigs parsley
½ teaspoon thyme
1 bay leaf
3 tablespoons butter
4 eggs
¼ teaspoon black pepper
Parsley for garnish

Wash brains in cold water; drain; remove membrane and any blood. Cover with cold water and let stand several hours; change water frequently. Drain. Cover with water; add vinegar, 1 teaspoon salt, peppercorns, onion, carrot, parsley, thyme, and bay leaf. Bring to a boil; lower heat and simmer 25 or 30 minutes.

Remove from heat. Let brains remain in cooking liquor until cool.

Drain; cut each brain in 3 pieces. Heat 2 tablespoons butter until lightly browned. Sauté brains 2 or 3 minutes; remove to hot dish. Add remaining butter to pan; scramble eggs; season with salt and pepper. Heap eggs on brains with parsley. Serves 4.

Maria Jeritza is one of Lüchow's favorite patrons. She always orders Viennese dishes, such as Schnitzel or Chicken Paprika; with her dinner she drinks champagne.

Writer Bob Considine is also a Schnitzel fan, but he drinks beer with the veal. So does his frequent guest, Louella Parsons, on her visits to New York. Marlene Dietrich chooses Vienna Backhendl—the delicious oven-baked chicken. She drinks Moselle with it.

Otto Harbach, president of ASCAP, which was founded at Lüchow's, calls the Wiener Schnitzel his favorite of all Lüchow meat dishes.

BAKED CALVES' BRAINS
GEBACKENES KALBSHIRN MIT GEMISCHTEM SALAT

> *3 calves' brains*
> *2 tablespoons vinegar*
> *1 teaspoon salt*
> *5 peppercorns*
> *½ onion, sliced*
> *1 small carrot, sliced*
> *4 sprigs parsley*
> *½ teaspoon thyme*
> *1 bay leaf*
> *1 egg, beaten with*
> *2 tablespoons water*

¾ cup flour
3 tablespoons butter
6 lemon slices

Wash brains in cold water; remove membrane and any blood. Cover with cold water; let stand several hours, changing water frequently.

Drain; put in saucepan with cold water to cover. Add vinegar, salt, peppercorns, onion, carrot, parsley, thyme, and bay leaf. Bring to a boil; lower heat and cook gently 25 to 30 minutes. Remove from heat; leave brains in cooking liquor until cool.

Drain; dip in egg, then in flour. Place in baking pan; sprinkle with lemon juice and brown in moderate oven (375° F.) until golden. Serve with garnish of sliced lemon and any favorite mixed green salad. Serves 6.

GOULASH

GYPSY GOULASH WITH SPÄTZLE

1 pound veal loin
1 pound lamb shoulder, boned
1 pound fresh pork shoulder, boned
2 small onions
2 tablespoons butter
2 tablespoons flour
1½ teaspoons salt
½ teaspoon pepper
½ teaspoon paprika
1 cup water
1 cup bouillon or stock
Hot Cooked Noodles (see recipe)

Wipe meat with damp cloth. Cut in 1½-inch pieces.

Slice onions. Heat butter in deep pot or Dutch oven and sauté onions until transparent. Add meat and cook 10 minutes. Sprinkle with flour; stir. Add seasonings, water, and bouillon. Increase water if necessary to cover meat. Cover pot; bring to a boil and boil 5 minutes. Lower heat and let cook slowly 1½ hours, or until meat is tender and liquid has cooked down to a thick sauce. Stir occasionally during cooking period. Serve garnished with Hot Cooked Noodles. Serves 6.

CREAM VEAL GOULASH WITH RICE
SAHNE GOULASCH MIT REIS

> *2½ pounds breast of veal, or boned shoulder*
> *2 quarts water*
> *¼ medium-size onion*
> *1½ teaspoons salt*
> *4 peppercorns*
> *2 cloves*
> *½ bay leaf*
> *3 tablespoons butter*
> *2 tablespoons flour*
> *2 cups stock from veal kettle*
> *¼ cup white wine*
> *1 cup cream*
> *2 egg yolks*
> *4 cups hot boiled rice*

Cut in serving-size pieces. Place in pot with water, onion, salt, peppercorns, cloves, and bay leaf. Cover; bring to a boil. Reduce heat and boil gently 1 hour.

Keep meat and broth hot, but not boiling, while you make gravy.

Melt butter; add flour and blend smoothly. Stir in broth and cook and stir until thickened. Add wine; stir and let boil 1 minute. Stir in cream and yolks. Remove from heat at once. Take meat from remaining broth; add to cream gravy. Serve on large platter surrounded by hot rice. Serves 6.

FILLET OF VEAL GOULASH À LA MINUTE WITH RICE

1 pound veal fillet
2 tablespoons butter
½ cup Paprika Sauce (see recipe)
2 cups hot boiled rice

Dice veal fine. Sauté in butter until golden and cooked. Place in small casserole; cover with Paprika Sauce. Heat to bubbling in hot oven (400° F.). Serve with hot rice. Serves 2 or 3.

GOULASH WITH SAUERKRAUT
SZEGEDINE GOULASCH

2 pounds veal or beef cut in 1½-inch squares
4 tablespoons beef suet or butter
1½ cups sliced onions
1 clove garlic, chopped
1 teaspoon salt
½ teaspoon pepper
1 cup chopped ripe or canned tomatoes, or tomato purée
1 cup sour cream
2 teaspoons paprika
2 teaspoons chopped caraway seeds
1 pound (2 cups) sauerkraut
2 or 3 tablespoons chopped parsley

Sauté meat in hot beef fat or butter until lightly browned. Add onions and cook 5 minutes. Add garlic, salt, pepper, tomatoes or tomato purée, and enough water barely to cover the mixture. Cook slowly until meat is nearly done and the sauce greatly reduced, about 45 minutes. Stir frequently. When sauce is cooked down, add sour cream, paprika, and caraway seeds. Simmer ½ hour longer.

Heat sauerkraut. Arrange alternate layers of goulash and sauerkraut in a warmed serving dish. Sprinkle top with parsley. Serves 8 or more.

> *Rachmaninoff, as is Toscanini, was a frequent guest at the Steinway family table. The famous pianist's favorite dish was Goulash with Sauerkraut. It is an Austrian version of goulash, and popular with many of our patrons.*

SAUSAGE

A mention of bratwurst to old-time managers and headwaiters at Lüchow's calls forth smiles and the name of Victor Herbert. He was responsible for making Lüchow's a favorite restaurant with many musicians, composers, and singers of his day. There is a special corner to Victor Herbert's memory, where he and a small group of his colleagues (including John Golden and Ray Hubbell) founded the American Society of Composers, Authors and Publishers. A bronze plaque commemorating the event, February 1914, hangs in this corner.

The composers lunched and dined often at the old Fourteenth Street restaurant, and cheese cake, German pancakes, and open apple cakes were all favorites. In those days the restaurant's baker was a Bavarian, and his celebrated recipes, which are still used here, were in great demand by Victor Herbert and his friends.

BLOOD SAUSAGE
BLUTWURST

>*3 pounds fresh fat pork belly*
>*1 pound fresh lean pork*
>*1 Spanish onion, chopped*
>*1½ teaspoons salt*
>*1 teaspoon pepper*
>*¼ teaspoon powdered cloves*
>*¼ teaspoon powdered ginger*
>*1 pint fresh pork blood*
>*Pork casings, washed and dried*

Cut half of the fat pork and all lean pork in small pieces; add onion. Cook over moderate heat until fat is flowing; then lower heat and cook 45 minutes. Add seasonings; mix. Grind coarsely.

Stir the fresh pork blood gradually into the meat mixture. Finely dice remaining fat pork and add; mix. Stuff into casings and tie. Cover with water. Bring to a boil; lower heat and simmer 25 minutes. Serves 8 or more.

BRATWURST AND SAUERKRAUT CASSEROLE
BRATWURST GASTRONOME

>*4 Broiled Bratwurst (see recipe)*
>*2 cups sauerkraut*
>*4 mushroom caps*
>*1 tablespoon butter*
>*1 cup Brown Sauce (see recipe)*

Broil bratwurst lightly. Place sauerkraut in baking dish; top with bratwurst. Chop mushrooms; sauté 3 minutes in butter. Pour over wurst and sauerkraut. Top with Brown Sauce. Heat under broiler until bubbling. Serves 4.

PORK AND LIVER SAUSAGE
LEBERWURST

> 2 pounds fresh fat pork belly
> ½ pound fresh pork shoulder
> 1½ pounds fresh pork liver, chopped
> 2 onions, sliced
> 1½ teaspoons salt
> ½ teaspoon pepper
> 1 teaspoon dried or fresh marjoram
> ½ teaspoon dried or fresh thyme
> Pork casings, washed and dried

Cut meat in small pieces. Combine with liver, onion, salt, and pepper. Simmer 40 minutes. Add herbs; stir. Grind all coarsely. Stuff into casings and tie. Cover with water; bring to a boil and boil 6 minutes. Serves 6 or more.

STRASSBOURG TRUFFLE SAUSAGE
STRASSBURGER TRÜFFEL LEBERWURST

> 2 pounds capon livers
> Milk to cover
> 1 medium-size onion, sliced
> ½ pound chicken fat
> 1½ pounds fat pork shoulder
> 1½ teaspoons salt
> ½ teaspoon pepper
> 1 teaspoon dried or fresh marjoram
> 4-ounce can truffles
> 4 tablespoons cognac
> Pork casings, washed and dried

Rinse livers; drain. Cover with milk; place in covered dish in refrigerator overnight.

Sauté onion in chicken fat; let cook slowly 20 minutes. Cut pork in small pieces; add to onion. Cook slowly, covered, at simmering point, 30 minutes. Add seasonings and drained livers. Grind very fine.

Cut truffles in small squares and add to mixture. Add cognac and mix well. Stuff into pork casings and tie. Barely cover with water. Bring to a boil, then lower heat and simmer 30 minutes. Serves 6 or more.

VEAL SAUSAGE
BOCKWURST

> *2 pounds veal*
> *1½ pounds pork shoulder*
> *1 pound pork suet*
> *1 pint heavy cream*
> *3 tablespoons minced chives*
> *1 onion, minced*
> *1½ teaspoons salt*
> *½ teaspoon pepper*
> *¼ teaspoon mace*
> *¼ teaspoon grated nutmeg*
> *Sheep casings, washed and dried*

Grind veal and pork 3 times. Chop suet fine. Combine the meat with suet, cream, chives, onion, and seasonings. Mix smoothly. Stuff into sheep casings. Tie in 4- or 5-inch lengths. Cover with hot water. Bring to a boil, then lower heat and simmer 15 minutes. Serves 10 or more.

PORK AND VEAL SAUSAGE
BRATWURST

> *½ pound fresh veal*
> *1 pound pork loin*
> *1½ teaspoons salt*
> *1 teaspoon pepper*
> *½ teaspoon grated nutmeg*
> *½ teaspoon mace*
> *Pork casings*

Combine all ingredients; put through grinder 3 times. Mix with about ½ cup water; fill pork casings. To serve, prepare:

Broiled Bratwurst: Cover bratwurst with hot water. Bring to a boil and remove from heat immediately. Let stand in the hot water a few minutes until firm. Drain; dip bratwurst in milk. Place in broiler and cook until golden brown under low-to-moderate heat. Serves 4.

GAME

BRAISED LEG CANADIAN HARE, SOUR CREAM SAUCE
HASENSCHLEGEL

> *Hindquarters dressed hare*
> *Salt and pepper*
> *6 thin slices bacon*
> *1 cup butter, melted*
> *1½ tablespoons flour*
> *1 cup sour cream*
> *2 tablespoons lemon juice*
> *1 cup hot water*

Split hindquarters of hare lengthwise in 2 pieces. Rinse; drain; pat dry. Rub well with salt and pepper. Arrange in baking pan with bacon slices over hare. Cook in hot oven (475° F.) 25 minutes. Lower heat to 350° F. Baste with melted butter and continue cooking 25 minutes. Sprinkle with flour; pour sour cream over all; add lemon juice and water. Cover and continue to cook about 20 minutes. Stir pan sauce occasionally. Test hare for tenderness. Let sauce thicken and cook down. Serves 2 to 4.

JUGGED HARE
HASENPFEFFER

> *2 legs and saddle of hare cut in 2 pieces*
> *1½ teaspoons salt*
> *4 tablespoons butter*
> *1 medium-size onion*
> *4 cloves*
> *1½ cups port wine or claret*
> *1 tablespoon lemon juice*
> *12 peppercorns*
> *1 herb bouquet (parsley, thyme, bay leaf)*
> *3 cups hot stock or bouillon*
> *2 tablespoons butter*
> *1 tablespoon flour*
> *Red currant jelly*

Rinse meat; pat dry; rub with salt. Sauté in 3 tablespoons butter until brown, about 30 minutes. Place in casserole; add onion stuck with cloves, ¾ cup wine, lemon juice, peppercorns, herbs, and stock. Cover and bake in moderate oven (350° F.) 2½ to 3 hours.

About ½ hour before serving, melt remaining tablespoon butter, blend with flour, and stir into hot mixture. Add remaining ¾ cup wine and any needed seasoning. Cover casserole again; cook 30 minutes.

Place pieces of hare on hot serving dish; strain gravy over them. Serve with red currant jelly. Serves 4.

Corey Ford's Lüchow favorite is Hasenpfeffer. He likes an imported dark beer with his meal.

LARDED SADDLE OF HARE
GESPICKTER HASENRÜCKEN

> *Saddle of hare, 2 to 2½ pounds*
> *Clove garlic*
> *3 tablespoons butter*
> *2½ teaspoons salt*
> *½ teaspoon paprika*
> *¼ teaspoon cayenne*
> *6 thin slices bacon or fat salt pork*
> *Sour Cream Sauce (see recipe)*
> *Orange slices*
> *Currant jelly*

Rinse meat; pat dry. Leave whole or cut in 4 pieces. Cut garlic and rub over all parts of saddle, then rub with butter. Sprinkle with salt, paprika, and cayenne. Place in roasting pan. Cover with bacon and salt pork. Roast uncovered in moderate oven (325° F.); allow 20 minutes per pound. When done, remove to warmed serving dish. Pour Sour Cream Sauce over; garnish with orange slices. Serve with currant jelly. Serves 4.

See recipe for Sour Cream Sauce and make it in the roasting pan after hare is removed. Strain; reheat.

Wild rice is usually served with this game.

This is a very popular dish, and during the season we may serve as many as 400 hare a day.

VENISON RAGOUT À LA LÜCHOW'S
REH RAGOUT

> *4 or 5 pounds venison shoulder*
> *Vinegar and red wine to cover*
> *2 onions, sliced*
> *2 carrots, sliced*
> *6 peppercorns*
> *1 tablespoon salt*
> *2 bay leaves*
> *2 tablespoons beef suet or lard*
> *1 cup red wine*
> *2 or 3 tablespoons flour*

Wipe venison with wet cloth. Cut in 1½-inch cubes. Place in enameled kettle or large crock; cover with a mixture of equal amounts of red wine and vinegar. Add onions, carrots, peppercorns, salt, and bay leaves. Cover and let stand in refrigerator 1 week.

When ready to cook, drain meat. Melt suet or lard in very hot heavy roasting pan. Place venison in pan and brown quickly in very hot oven (475° F. to 500° F.) 20 to 30 minutes. Add onions and carrots from the marinade (do not use marinade liquid). Add 1 cup red wine and sufficient water to cover venison. Lower oven heat to moderate (350° F.), or just hot enough to simmer liquid in pan. Cook 2½ to 3 hours. Remove any excess fat.

Place venison on hot serving dish. Stir enough flour into pan to make a smooth gravy; bring to a boil on top of range, stir, then strain over venison. Serves 8.

> *When Theodore Roosevelt dined at Lüchow's he ordered game. One of his favorite dishes was venison, with which he usually had a bottle of Pommard. Venison was also a favorite of Sigmund Romberg. He liked Würzburger beer with his roast.*

FILET MIGNON OF VENISON, HUNTER STYLE

3 pounds venison steak
1 teaspoon salt
4 peppercorns
1 medium-size onion, sliced
1 carrot, sliced
4 sprigs parsley
½ teaspoon thyme
1 bay leaf
½ cup white wine
½ cup olive oil
Sour Cream Sauce
Purée of Lentils (see recipe)
Red Cabbage (see recipe)

Have leg or loin of venison cut in steaks about ¾ inch thick.
Season with salt. Place in bowl. Mix peppercorns, onion, carrot,
parsley, thyme, bay leaf, wine, and 5 tablespoons olive oil and

pour over steaks. Cover and let stand in refrigerator 24 hours. Turn meat in marinade from time to time.

Remove meat from marinade; pat dry. Heat 3 tablespoons olive oil; cook venison 3 minutes on each side—longer if meat is preferred well done. Remove meat to a warmed serving dish and keep it hot. Make sauce in same pan. Serves 4.

SOUR CREAM SAUCE:

> *2 tablespoons butter*
> *2 tablespoons flour*
> *2 shallots, chopped*
> *4 tablespoons white wine*
> *2 peppercorns, crushed fine*
> *1 cup sour cream*
> *Salt*
> *Pepper*
> *Juice ½ lemon*

Pour off excess fat from pan in which venison cooked. Melt butter in pan; stir flour and shallots smoothly in and mix well, stirring into them all the browned fat of the pan. Add wine, peppercorns gradually; mix well after each addition. Add cream and a little salt and pepper if needed. Cook and stir continually till thickened. Before serving, add lemon juice if desired. Pour over meat and serve at once. Serves 4.

Purée of Lentils and Red Cabbage are served with this dish.

VENISON STEW WITH POTATO DUMPLINGS
REH RAGOUT

> *3 pounds venison shoulder*
> *4 tablespoons butter*
> *4 tablespoons flour*
> *1½ teaspoons salt*
> *2 cups stock or bouillon*

4 cups hot water
1 small onion, sliced
6 peppercorns
2 cloves
1 bay leaf
Juice ½ lemon
½ cup red wine
Potato Dumplings (*see recipe*)

Rinse meat; wipe dry. Cut in serving-size pieces. Heat butter in deep kettle. Stir flour smoothly in and cook until browned. Add salt, stock, hot water; stir and mix well. Add onion, peppercorns, cloves, bay leaf, and lemon juice. Bring to a boil and let boil 5 minutes. Add meat. Cover pot; boil gently 1½ hours Add wine and mix with gravy in pot; continue cooking 15 min utes. Serve with Potato Dumplings. Serves 6.

6.

CHEESE AND EGGS

Cheeses are like wine in one respect: their age is most important to them. And, too, they complement each other. Our cheese assortment comes from the best American and foreign markets, purchased according to age and tasted to make sure they are just right before they go into the storerooms.

Lüchow's patrons find themselves in a cheese heaven when they consult the menu. There are such standards as Roquefort, old Cheddar with sherry, camembert, and both domestic and imported Swiss, as well as Liederkranz and Limburger, heralded by their heady fumes as they emerge into the dining room. These are offset by the mild cheeses, Philadelphia cream and pot cheese, delicious with Bar-le-Duc, or the imported lingonberries and *Preisselbeeren*. Imported bleu cheese has been added recently, and a stout Canadian oka. Both are favorites on the cold-cut platter and with salads.

An order of cheese includes the diner's choice of English plain biscuits, American salty crackers, toasted rolls, or anything else the hungry man may desire.

A favorite supper dish at Lüchow's is Welsh rarebit, or its more substantial version, a Golden Buck, served from a chafing dish at the table.

We offer nearly every variety of egg dish, but those most in demand are the familiar scrambles and omelets, because they go best with German and Austrian meat, game, and fowl specialties.

OMELETS

4 eggs
¼ teaspoon salt
1 tablespoon butter
Parsley

Lightly beat eggs and salt with fork. Heat butter in frying pan until lightly browned; pour eggs into pan. Stir briskly with fork. Shake skillet to loosen bottom of omelet from pan. Fold omelet in half; tilt pan over warmed serving dish and slip omelet onto it. Garnish with parsley. Serves 2.

Serve fried potatoes, asparagus tips, sautéed mushrooms, or peas with omelet.

Spanish Omelet: Fold 2 or 3 tablespoons Creole Sauce in omelet; also add 1 or 2 tablespoons sauce to top.

Omelet with Mushroom Sauce: Serve 2 or 3 tablespoons Mushroom Sauce over omelet.

Mushroom Omelet: Sauté 3 tablespoons sliced fresh mushrooms in 1 teaspoon butter. Mix with eggs which have been slightly beaten. Garnish omelet with a few whole mushrooms sautéed in butter.

Dessert Omelet: Make plain omelet. Before folding, sprinkle generously with powdered sugar and add 1 or 2 tablespoons jam or marmalade; fold. While omelet is cooking, heat 3 tablespoons rum. Slip omelet onto warmed plate; sprinkle with sugar; pour hot rum over. Light rum, and spoon over omelet as it flames. Serve flaming.

SCRAMBLED EGGS

> 6 eggs
> 2 tablespoons cream
> ½ teaspoon salt
> 1 tablespoon butter
> 4 slices buttered toast
> Parsley

Beat eggs with cream and salt. Heat butter in frying pan and pour eggs in. Stir slowly; let cook until firm. Heap on slices of toast. Garnish with parsley. Serves 4.

Variations: Serve crisply broiled bacon or sautéed mushrooms with eggs. Or add 2 tablespoons minced mushrooms to egg and cream mixture before cooking.

SCRAMBLED EGGS WITH CHICKEN LIVERS

Add 2 chopped, cooked chicken livers to each 2 scrambled eggs. Cook with eggs or use as garnish around scrambled eggs on toast.

LÜCHOW'S WELSH RAREBIT

> 1 pound quick-melting yellow cheese
> 1 tablespoon butter
> 1 cup beer
> 1 whole egg, beaten
> 1 teaspoon Worcestershire sauce
> 1 teaspoon salt
> ½ teaspoon paprika
> ¼ teaspoon dry mustard
> 4 slices buttered toast

Grate cheese. Melt butter in chafing-dish pan over hot water; add beer, stirring. When beer is warm, stir in cheese with a fork until cheese is melted. Beat in egg and seasonings. Spoon at once onto toast. Serves 4.

Golden Buck: Fry or poach 4 eggs; place 1 on each serving of Rarebit.

7.

DUMPLINGS AND NOODLES

Dumplings are one of the particular glories of the German cuisine. We consider them, along with noodles, as an accompaniment without which many dishes on our menu would seem incomplete.

Yet when one observes the Kartoffel Klösse, white and succulent, resting on the plate, there is a temptation to regard them as a course in themselves. In combination with the meats they complement, dumplings become part of a harmonious whole. In the recipes which follow, we show you the several variations it is possible to play upon the theme.

Of noodles, it need only be said that of all the infinite varieties of goulash which exist in the world, our Goulash Spätzle, sautéed to a golden turn, is a tribute to the creative imagination of the chef who first transformed this common and lowly dish into a culinary delight.

DUMPLINGS FOR BOILED BEEF

2 cups sifted flour
1 teaspoon salt

4 teaspoons baking powder
¼ teaspoon pepper
1 egg, beaten
3 tablespoons shortening, melted
Milk
4 to 8 cups beef stock or broth

Sift dry ingredients together. Add egg and shortening and beat smoothly. Add enough milk to make a fairly moist batter.

Drop by spoonfuls into boiling beef kettle or into boiling broth or stock. Cover tightly; boil 15 to 18 minutes. Serves 6.

POTATO DUMPLINGS I
KARTOFFEL KLÖSSE

> *3 pounds (9) medium-size potatoes*
> *3 egg yolks, beaten*
> *3 tablespoons cornstarch*
> *3 tablespoons raw farina or Cream of Wheat*
> *½ teaspoon pepper*
> *1½ teaspoons salt*
> *¼ teaspoon grated nutmeg*
> *1 cup toasted or fried white bread cubes*
> *Flour*
> *1½ quarts boiling salted water (1½ teaspoons salt)*

Scrub potatoes. Boil in salted water until just soft enough to mash. Drain and mash smoothly. Add egg yolks, cornstarch, cereal, pepper, salt, and nutmeg. Beat well; shape into dumplings; place few bread cubes in center of each. (It is a good idea to shape 1 dumpling first, and if it does not hold together while cooking, beat a little flour into dumpling mixture before shaping remainder.)

Roll each dumpling lightly in flour. Cook in rapidly boiling salted water 15 to 20 minutes. Remove cooked dumplings from water; serve hot. Makes 12 or more dumplings, serves 6 to 8.

NOTE: Any leftover dumplings may be cut in half, sautéed in butter, and used as garnish on a meat or salad platter.

POTATO DUMPLINGS II
KARTOFFEL KLÖSSE

> *2 pounds (6) raw potatoes*
> *4 slices white bread*
> *1 teaspoon salt*
> *¼ teaspoon pepper*

1 onion, grated
1 teaspoon minced parsley
2 eggs, well beaten
¼ cup flour
1½ quarts boiling salted water

Wash, peel, and grate potatoes. Soak bread in a little cold water; squeeze out as much water as possible. Mix bread, salt, pepper, onions, and parsley. Add potatoes and eggs; mix well.

Form into balls; roll lightly in flour; drop into salted boiling water (1 teaspoon salt to each quart water). Cover pot tightly; boil 15 minutes. Serve with sauerkraut, beef, or chicken. Serves 4 or more.

LIVER DUMPLINGS
LEBER KLÖSSE

½ pound fresh pork belly
½ pound beef kidney fat
1 pound calves' liver
1 onion, sliced
1 teaspoon butter
12 slices white bread (without crusts)
1 cup heavy cream
2 eggs, beaten
1½ teaspoons salt
½ teaspoon pepper
¼ teaspoon grated nutmeg
1 clove garlic, mashed
Flour
1 quart boiling stock or bouillon
2 tablespoons crumbs
4 tablespoons butter

Grind pork, fat, and liver coarsely together. Cook onion lightly in butter; add to meat. Soak bread in cream and eggs and add all to meat mixture. Add seasonings and garlic. Beat smoothly. If too soft to hold shape on a spoon, beat a little flour into mixture.

Drop from spoon into boiling stock and boil 20 minutes. Lift out on wire strainer or slotted spoon. Place on hot dish; sprinkle with crumbs browned in butter. Serves 8 or more.

GOULASH SPÄTZLE

> *1 pound (3¼ cups) sifted flour*
> *1 teaspoon salt*
> *½ teaspoon grated nutmeg*
> *4 eggs, beaten*
> *Milk*
> *2 quarts boiling salted water*
> *4 or 5 tablespoons butter*
> *½ cup toasted bread crumbs*

Sift dry ingredients together. Beat eggs in. Add milk gradually to make heavy dough. Force through large-hole colander into kettle of rapidly boiling salted water. (Use 1 teaspoon salt to 1 quart water.) Boil 6 to 8 minutes.

Remove Spätzle with large strainer-spoon and put in colander. Dash with cold water; drain. Sauté in butter until golden. Sprinkle with crumbs and serve. Serves 6 or more.

FRIED SPÄTZLE WITH EGGS

> *Spätzle (See Goulash Spätzle)*
> *3 tablespoons butter*
> *2 eggs, beaten*

Sauté half of the drained, freshly made Spätzle in butter. When lightly browned, add eggs, mix, and finish cooking like omelet. When bottom is brown, fold and serve. Serves 2 to 4.

LIVER DUMPLINGS AND SAUERKRAUT
LEBER KLÖSSE MIT SAUERKRAUT

1 pound fresh beef
1 pound fresh pork loin
½ pound fresh veal
½ pound fresh pork or calves' liver
2 tablespoons chopped shallots
2 cloves garlic, chopped
2 eggs, beaten
1 teaspoon salt
½ teaspoon pepper
1 teaspoon Worcestershire sauce
Boiling water
3 pounds sauerkraut, heated
6 onions sliced thin, fried in
2 tablespoons butter

Grind beef, pork, veal, and liver together twice. Combine with shallots, garlic, eggs, and seasonings. Stir until mixture is well blended. Form into small balls. Cook in salted boiling water 10 minutes. (Water must be boiling rapidly; add 1 teaspoon salt to each quart of water.)

Lift liver balls out on slotted spoon. Serve on hot sauerkraut garnished with fried onions. Serves 6 or more.

8.

SALADS AND SALAD DRESSINGS

Sometimes a diner roams the precincts of our menu looking for a favorite German dish under the salad heading and finds it listed with the appetizers. That is one of the peculiarities of a German menu, which is admirable in most other respects. Cold meat, game, fowl in aspic, or a herring and potato mixture is often found under the salads, the appetizers, or both.

For those who enjoy the modern tossed green and other light salads, we are happy to mix these dishes with the excellent dressings devised by our chefs. For those who have a special affection for German cuisine, there are the hearty potato salads, head lettuce with Roquefort cheese, and cucumbers in sour cream or vinaigrette.

CHICKEN SALAD

4 cups coarsely cut cooked chicken
½ cup sliced mushrooms
1 teaspoon butter
2 tablespoons sliced truffles
2 cups mayonnaise

1 cup chopped celery
1 cup heavy cream
Crisp lettuce, ripe olives, tomato quarters, capers

The pieces of chicken should be 1 inch long or larger. Sauté mushrooms 2 or 3 minutes in butter; let cool. Combine with chicken; add truffles and enough mayonnaise to coat mixture. Put in glass or china bowl; let stand covered in refrigerator 1 hour or longer. Add celery and mix well. Whip cream; combine with salad. Heap on crisp lettuce. Garnish with black olives, tomato quarters, and few capers. Serves 4 or more.

KNOB CELERY SALAD

1½ pounds knob (root) celery
Boiling salted water
Mayonnaise
1 teaspoon prepared mustard
Sliced pickled beets

Wash celery root; peel; cut in julienne pieces. Cover with boiling salted water. Boil until tender, about 5 minutes. Drain; let cool.

Mix mayonnaise with mustard; combine with celery root. Garnish with sliced pickled beets. Serves 4.

Variation: An old German recipe for this salad:

5 tablespoons olive oil
6 tablespoons vinegar
1 teaspoon salt
1 tablespoon sugar
¼ teaspoon pepper
½ cup bouillon

Mix all ingredients; pour over warm cooked celery root. Chill 1 hour before serving. Serves 4.

LÜCHOW'S COLE SLAW

1 head white cabbage
2 quarts boiling water
2 onions, shredded fine
1 or 2 green peppers, shredded fine
¼ cup vinegar
2 egg yolks, beaten
1 teaspoon salt
½ teaspoon pepper
3 tablespoons olive oil
1 cup sour cream

Wash cabbage; slice or cut fine. Scald 5 minutes and drain well through colander; press out all water. Mix with onions, green peppers, and vinegar. Beat eggs, salt, and pepper together; add oil gradually, beating steadily. Pour over cabbage mixture; stir well. Pour sour cream over and stir until evenly mixed. Serves 4 to 6.

CUCUMBERS IN SOUR CREAM

2 large cucumbers
1 tablespoon salt
1 cup thick sour cream
2 tablespoons vinegar
½ teaspoon black pepper
½ teaspoon chopped chives or dill

Wash cucumbers; scrape or peel; slice very thin. Place in glass or china bowl; sprinkle with salt. Let stand 1 hour or a little longer. Squeeze liquid out of cucumbers. Combine remaining ingredients and pour over cucumbers. Mix and serve. Serves 4.

CUCUMBER VINAIGRETTE SALAD

2 large cucumbers
1 tablespoon salt
3 tablespoons olive oil
4 tablespoons vinegar
½ teaspoon freshly ground black pepper
1 tablespoon minced parsley

Wash cucumbers; scrape or peel; slice very thin. Place in glass or china bowl; sprinkle with salt. Let stand 1 hour or longer. Squeeze liquid out of cucumbers. Combine remaining ingredients. Pour over cucumbers. Mix and serve. Serves 4.

HOT POTATO SALAD WITH BACON

SPECK SALAT

1 pound (3 medium) potatoes
6 slices bacon, diced
1 medium-size onion, diced
½ cup vinegar
½ cup stock or bouillon
1 teaspoon salt
¼ teaspoon pepper
1 teaspoon sugar
1 egg yolk, beaten

Scrub potatoes; rinse. Boil in jackets; let cool. Peel and cut in ¼-inch slices.

Cook bacon in hot pan until crisp. Add onion; stir and cook until transparent. Add vinegar, stock or bouillon, and seasonings. Stir; let come to a boil. Stir in egg; remove from heat and pour over potatoes. Serves 2 to 4.

LÜCHOW'S POTATO SALAD

> *2 pounds (6) potatoes*
> *½ cup beef or chicken stock*
> *½ onion, chopped*
> *6 tablespoons wine vinegar*
> *6 tablespoons olive oil*
> *1 teaspoon salt*
> *½ teaspoon freshly ground pepper*
> *1 egg yolk*

Wash and scrub potatoes; boil in jackets until tender. Let cool only enough to peel and slice. Pour stock over to be absorbed by potatoes; add onion. Mix remaining ingredients; beat smoothly together. Pour over potatoes. Serve warm or chilled. Serves 4.

POTATO SALAD WITH SOUR CREAM DRESSING

> *2 pounds (6) potatoes*
> *Boiling water*
> *1 pint thick sour cream*
> *¼ cup vinegar*
> *1 tablespoon sugar*
> *1 teaspoon salt*
> *¼ teaspoon pepper*
> *Paprika*

Scrub potatoes, rinse. Cover with boiling water; boil until tender, 25 to 30 minutes. Let cool slightly. Slice in jackets. Combine remaining ingredients; pour over potatoes, mix. Sprinkle with paprika and serve. Serves 4 to 6.

LOBSTER SALAD

> *Meat of 3 freshly boiled lobsters*
> *3 tablespoons vinegar*
> *4 tablespoons oil*
> *1 teaspoon salt*
> *¼ teaspoon pepper*
> *1 cup mayonnaise*
> *Crisp curly lettuce*
> *Capers, radishes, black olives*

Cut lobster meat in good-size pieces. Place in glass or china bowl. Mix vinegar, oil, salt, and pepper and pour over meat. Cover and let stand in refrigerator about 1 hour. Combine with mayonnaise; heap on lettuce. Garnish with few capers, radishes, and ripe olives. Serves 4 to 6.

LÜCHOW'S COLD HERB DRESSING

> *2 hard-cooked eggs*
> *1 raw egg yolk*
> *½ cup olive oil*
> *1 tablespoon minced mixed herbs (parsley,*
>   *orégano, thyme, chives)*
> *½ teaspoon dry mustard*
> *1½ teaspoons lemon juice or vinegar*
> *½ teaspoon salt*
> *¼ teaspoon pepper*

Chop egg whites. Mash yolks and beat with raw yolk; add oil, a few drops at a time. Add herbs, mustard, lemon juice or vinegar, salt, and pepper. Beat well. Add chopped egg white last. Makes about ¾ cup dressing. Serves 6.

LÜCHOW'S ROQUEFORT DRESSING

> *1 cup imported olive oil*
> *½ cup crumbled or diced imported Roquefort cheese*
> *¼ cup freshly squeezed lemon juice*

Mix just before serving on tossed green salad. Serves 4.

LÜCHOW'S MAYONNAISE

> *4 fresh egg yolks*
> *½ teaspoon salt*
> *⅛ teaspoon black pepper*
> *1 teaspoon dry mustard*
> *1 tablespoon wine vinegar*
> *2 cups fine olive oil*

Beat yolks with salt, pepper, and mustard. Add a few drops vinegar; beat smoothly. Add oil drop by drop, mixing well all the time. Add few drops vinegar; then alternate oil and vinegar until all is added and beaten smoothly together. Use at once. If stored in refrigerator, beat gently before serving. Makes 2½ to 3 cups.

LÜCHOW'S TARTARE SAUCE

> *1 quart Lüchow's Mayonnaise*
> *½ onion*
> *1 shallot*
> *½ bunch parsley, washed and dried*
> *½ bunch chives*
> *1 sour pickle*
> *1 sweet pickle*
> *1 oz. capers*
> *1 hard-boiled egg*

Chop all ingredients fine, and mix into the Mayonnaise. Season to taste with salt, pepper, and lemon juice.

$9.$

VEGETABLES

Buying vegetables for a restaurant is an art which might well awe the average housewife. Lüchow's buyer must know how to choose among the wholesale arrays of farm produce displayed daily to restaurateurs, a task immensely complicated by the fact that a great many grades and qualities of every vegetable are available from day to day. Naturally, Lüchow's man selects only the top quality in any vegetable.

Asparagus must come from California or Pennsylvania, because that vegetable grows most tender and flavorful in these two garden spots. String beans must be flat and green. Carrots must come from the West Coast, because they are sweeter. This is also true of iceberg lettuce.

Large onions destined for salads, marinades, and ragouts in Lüchow's kitchen come from New Mexico and Texas. Spinach from southern Virginia is greener and has a better flavor. Idaho potatoes are best for baking, but the season qualifies potatoes and sweet potatoes from several other sections of the country for our table.

Sweet corn, bought from nearby farms, must be very young and as fresh as possible. Dried vegetables like lentils, beans, and peas used in soups are as carefully chosen for quality as their fresh brothers in the green department.

FRIED APPLES AND ONIONS

> *6 large tart apples*
> *2 onions*
> *2 tablespoons butter or bacon drippings*
> *1 teaspoon salt*
> *½ teaspoon paprika*
> *½ cup sugar*

Wash and core apples. Cut in thick slices, unpeeled.

Wash, peel, and slice onions. Heat butter or drippings in frying pan. Spread layer of onions in hot fat. Cook slowly 5 minutes. Season with salt and paprika. Cover with layer of apples; season with sugar and salt. Cover pan until steaming, then lower heat and cook 10 minutes, or until apples are nearly tender. Uncover and continue cooking. Add additional butter or a little hot water if needed. Serves 6.

RED CABBAGE

> *1 head red cabbage, sliced thin*
> *2 onions, sliced*
> *2 apples, cored and sliced*
> *½ cup red currant jelly*
> *1 bay leaf*
> *Salt*
> *Dash of pepper*
> *¼ pound butter, chicken, or bacon fat*
> *4 medium-size ham knuckles*
> *3 ounces vinegar*

Mix red cabbage with onions, apples, currant jelly, bay leaf, salt, and pepper.

Put butter, chicken, or bacon fat in heavy casserole with tight-fitting cover; add red cabbage, ham knuckles, ¼ cup water. Bring to a boil and cook slowly 2½ hours. Add vinegar at the last minute; remove bay leaf. Serves 6.

RED CABBAGE WITH APPLES
ROT KRAUT MIT ÄPFELN

> *1 medium-size head red cabbage*
> *1 or 2 tart apples*
> *2 tablespoons chicken fat*
> *1 medium-size onion, sliced*
> *1 quart water*
> *½ cup light vinegar (red wine vinegar preferred)*
> *½ cup sugar*
> *½ teaspoon salt*
> *¼ teaspoon pepper*
> *2 cloves*
> *1 bay leaf*
> *Juice ½ lemon*
> *2 or 3 tablespoons flour*

Wash cabbage, drain; cut as for Cole Slaw.

Wash and core apples; peel and cut in small pieces.

Heat chicken fat in large saucepan and sauté onion and apples 3 or 4 minutes. Add water, vinegar, sugar, salt, pepper, cloves, bay leaf, and lemon juice. Stir; bring to a boil. Add cabbage. Cover and let simmer 45 minutes, or until tender. Just before serving, sprinkle flour on top to absorb liquid. Serves 4.

BRAISED CELERY

> *12 tender stalks celery*
> *1½ cups boiling stock or bouillon*
> *½ teaspoon salt*
> *¼ teaspoon pepper*
> *2 tablespoons butter*
> *½ teaspoon flour*
> *Paprika*

Wash and peel celery; cut in 3-inch lengths; remove all leaves. Cover with boiling stock. If bouillon is not spicy enough, add salt and pepper. Simmer covered until tender, about 20 minutes. Drain; reserve stock.

Heat butter; stir flour in and cook until browned. Add stock; cook and stir until boiling. Add celery. Cook a few minutes to reduce liquid. Serves 4.

BOILED CHESTNUTS

> *1½ pounds chestnuts*
> *2 cups boiling salted water or stock*
> *2 stalks celery, chopped*
> *2 tablespoons butter*
> *¼ teaspoon pepper*
> *¼ cup hot cream*
> *Paprika*

Cover chestnuts with cold water; bring to a boil. Boil 30 minutes. Drain; plunge nuts in cold water. Loosen hulls with paring knife and rub skins from nuts with coarse towel.

Cover nuts with boiling salted water or stock; add celery; cook until tender, 25 minutes. Leave chestnuts in stock to cool.

To serve separately as vegetable, drain boiled chestnuts; mash with butter, pepper, and cream. Whip like mashed potatoes. Heap in serving dish; sprinkle lightly with paprika. Serves 4.

To use as garnish on cooked greens or other dishes, drain boiled chestnuts; chop or cut coarsely. Combine with cooked greens or use on top as garnish. (See Green Kale with Chestnuts.)

SAVORY GREEN BEANS

> *2 pounds fresh green beans*
> *2 tablespoons butter or drippings*

> *3 cups bouillon or stock*
> *1 tablespoon flour*
> *1 teaspoon sugar*
> *1 teaspoon salt*
> *2 tablespoons vinegar*
> *1 small piece summer savory*
> *1 tablespoon chopped parsley*

Wash beans; break off tips and remove strings; cut or break in 4 pieces each. Place in saucepan with butter or drippings and bouillon; cook covered 25 minutes, or until tender. Add more bouillon if necessary. When nearly done, sprinkle beans with flour, sugar, salt, and vinegar. Cook uncovered a few minutes more. Sprinkle with herbs and serve. Serves 6.

GREEN KALE WITH CHESTNUTS

> *3 pounds fresh kale*
> *2 quarts boiling salted water*
> *6 tablespoons butter*
> *2 tablespoons flour*
> *2 cups bouillon*
> *1 teaspoon salt*
> *½ teaspoon pepper*
> *¼ teaspoon grated nutmeg*
> *½ teaspoon paprika*
> *½ cup sweet cream*
> *1 cup chopped Boiled Chestnuts (see recipe)*

Wash kale several times; drain. Cut rib from leaves; wash again; drain. Cover with boiling salted water and cook 30 minutes, or until tender. Drain in colander. Chop fine or rub through colander.

Melt butter; stir flour into it; add bouillon, salt, pepper, nutmeg, and paprika. Cook and stir until boiling. Add kale; cook slowly 20 minutes, or until little liquid remains. Stir cream and chestnuts in; heat 1 or 2 minutes. Or use chestnuts on top as garnish. Serves 6.

PURÉE OF LENTILS

> 2 cups dried lentils
> 4 cups bouillon or stock
> 1 slice smoked sausage or salt pork
> 2 sprigs parsley
> 1 or 2 small onions, sliced
> 1 clove garlic
> 1 bay leaf
> 2 cloves
> 2 tablespoons butter
> ¼ cup heavy cream
> ½ teaspoon salt
> ¼ teaspoon pepper

Wash lentils; drain. Cover with cold water; let soak overnight. Drain. Cover with bouillon or stock; add sausage or salt pork. Place parsley, onions, garlic, bay leaf, and cloves in loose cheese-cloth bag and add to kettle. Bring slowly to a boil; lower heat and cook slowly until lentils are tender, about 1½ hours. Remove herb bag after first hour of cooking. Add boiling water or stock if lentils cook too quickly.

When lentils are done, put through fine sieve or strainer. Set over heat and whip butter, cream, and seasonings into the purée. Serves 4.

NEW LIMA BEANS IN CREAM

> 1 quart shelled young lima beans
> Boiling water

1 slice bacon, diced
1 teaspoon salt
1 cup heavy cream
1½ tablespoons lemon juice
1 tablespoon minced parsley

Wash beans; drain. Barely cover with boiling water. Add bacon. Cover beans and cook 15 minutes. Add salt and cook uncovered over higher heat until most of water evaporates. Add cream; stir lemon juice and parsley in and serve when steaming hot. Do not let boil after cream is added. Serves 4.

MUSHROOMS IN SOUR CREAM

2 pounds fresh mushrooms
¼ pound butter
1 medium-size onion, peeled
1 tablespoon flour
1 cup sour cream
½ teaspoon meat extract
1 teaspoon salt
½ teaspoon pepper
1 tablespoon minced parsley

Wash mushrooms; break off stems; peel any heavy caps; slice in quarters. Sauté in hot butter a few minutes. Add onion; cover pan and cook gently 15 to 20 minutes. Remove onion. Sprinkle flour on mushrooms; stir lightly. Add cream, meat extract, salt, and pepper; mix. Heat a few minutes, but do not let boil. Sprinkle with parsley and serve. Serves 6.

NEW PEAS WITH ONIONS, FINES HERBES

1 pound fresh young peas
6 young scallions

½ teaspoon salt
Dash of pepper
1 tablespoon sugar
2 tablespoons butter
1 teaspoon flour
¾ cup boiling water
1 tablespoon mixed parsley, tarragon, chives, and
    chervil

Wash and shell peas. Wash scallions; cut white part in 1-inch lengths. Combine with peas in small casserole. Add salt, pepper, and sugar. Mix butter and flour and add water. Cover and cook in moderate oven (375° F.) until peas are tender, about 30 minutes. Stir herbs into peas. Serve from casserole. Serves 3 or 4.

COTTAGE FRIED POTATOES

5 raw potatoes
2 tablespoons bacon drippings or other fat
1 teaspoon salt
¼ teaspoon black pepper

Slice potatoes; fry in hot fat. Season with salt and pepper. Serves 4.

GERMAN FRIED POTATOES

4 or 5 cold boiled potatoes
½ tablespoon salt
2 tablespoons butter
½ teaspoon paprika

Slice potatoes; season with salt. Sauté in butter until light brown. Turn frequently with spatula or pancake turner. Sprinkle with paprika. Serves 4.

LYONNAISE POTATOES

4 or 5 boiled potatoes
2 or 3 tablespoons butter
½ onion, minced
2 tablespoons minced parsley

Peel and slice potatoes thin. Sauté in butter slowly until golden. Remove potatoes, leaving butter in pan. Add onion and cook 3 or 4 minutes. Return potatoes to pan and mix gently with onion; cook 1 or 2 minutes more. Serve sprinkled with parsley. Serves 3 or 4.

BETWEEN-THE-ACTS POTATOES

5 raw potatoes
Deep fat
Salt

Peel and cut potatoes 3 inches long, ¼ inch thick. Wash and dry. Fry in deep fat until cooked and golden brown. Season with salt. Serves 5.

POTATOES AU GRATIN

2 cups hot mashed potatoes
¼ cup grated cheese
2 tablespoons melted butter

Spread potatoes in lightly buttered au gratin dish (shallow casserole or baking dish). Sprinkle generously with cheese and melted butter. Place in hot oven (400° F.) or under moderate broiler heat until golden brown. Serves 4.

Variation: Dice cold boiled potatoes fine. Boil in cream 6 minutes. Season well with salt and pepper. Pour into au gratin dish. Sprinkle top with grated cheese. Brown in hot oven (400° F.) until golden and crusty.

POTATOES PARISIENNE

> *8 large new potatoes*
> *Boiling salted water*
> *2 tablespoons butter or bacon drippings*
> *Salt*
> *Paprika*

Wash potatoes; peel. Cover with cold water and let stand 1 hour. Drain; cut into balls with French cutter. Cover with boiling salted water and cook until almost tender, 25 minutes. Drain.

Melt butter or drippings in frying pan; cook potatoes until light brown. Season with salt and paprika. Place in shallow pan in hot oven (400° F.) to crisp and brown. Add more butter if needed. Serves 6.

LÜCHOW'S POTATO PANCAKES
KARTOFFEL PFANNKUCHEN

> *2 pounds (6) medium-size potatoes*
> *½ medium-size onion, grated*
> *2 tablespoons flour*
> *2 eggs, beaten*
> *1½ teaspoons salt*
> *¼ teaspoon pepper*
> *¼ teaspoon grated nutmeg*
> *2 tablespoons minced parsley*
> *3 or 4 tablespoons butter*
> *4 strips crisply cooked bacon*

Wash and peel potatoes. Cover with cold water; drain. Grate at once and drain water that collects on grated potatoes. Add onion and mix. Add flour, eggs, salt, pepper, nutmeg, and parsley. Mix thoroughly.

Heat butter on griddle or in large frying pan. Place large spoonfuls of potato mixture in hot pan; bake 3 or 4 pancakes at one time until brown and crisp on each side, turning with pancake turner. Place on hot dish. Garnish with crisp bacon. Serves 6.

Serve stewed apples with these pancakes.

BAKED SAUERKRAUT WITH APPLES
WEINKRAUT

> *1 quart sauerkraut*
> *¼ cup sliced onion*
> *2 tablespoons butter or bacon drippings*
> *2 or 3 medium-size apples*
> *1½ cups white wine*
> *½ cup stock or bouillon*
> *1 teaspoon brown sugar*
> *1 teaspoon celery seed*

Drain kraut slightly. Cook onion in butter or drippings until transparent. Add sauerkraut; stir; cook slowly.

Wash, peel, and core apples; dice fruit and add to sauerkraut. Add wine and enough stock or bouillon to cover. Cook slowly, uncovered, 30 minutes. Add sugar and celery seed; cover and finish cooking in moderate oven (325° F.) 30 minutes longer. Serves 4 to 6.

BOILED TURNIPS

> *8 medium-size white turnips*
> *1 quart boiling salted water*
> *3 tablespoons butter*
> *1 tablespoon flour*

½ *cup bouillon*
½ *teaspoon salt*

Wash, peel, and quarter or slice turnips. Barely cover with salted boiling water and cook uncovered until tender, 20 minutes or longer. Let water cook down. Add butter; sprinkle flour over turnips. Add bouillon and seasonings. Cook 15 minutes. Serves 4.

Variation: Prepare yellow turnips the same way. When done, mash turnips; beat butter and seasonings into them. Sprinkle with few grains black pepper.

WILD RICE WITH RAISINS

1 cup wild rice
½ *cup minced onion*
1 tablespoon butter
3 cups boiling stock
½ *cup seedless raisins*
Boiling water

Wash rice; drain; let dry. Sauté onion in butter; stir rice into it; cook 3 or 4 minutes. Add stock. Cover; cook slowly, without stirring, 30 minutes, or until rice is tender and stock absorbed.

Cover raisins with boiling water; let stand until plump. Drain; stir into rice. Serves 4.

LEIPZIGER ALLERLEI

¼ *pound fresh lima beans*
¼ *pound fresh string beans, cut*
¼ *pound fresh peas*
1 small head cauliflower cut in flowerets
¼ *pound mushrooms (Steinpilze), sliced*
¼ *pound sweet butter*

2 tablespoons flour
1 cup fresh cream
Salt, pepper, nutmeg
2 egg yolks

Cook all the fresh vegetables; drain; keep hot. Melt butter; blend in flour; add heated cream; let simmer 5 minutes. Beat the egg yolks with tablespoon of cream and add to the sauce. Pour sauce over vegetables and mix altogether, including seasoning. Serves 4.

10.

SAUCES

Sauces are at once the triumph and despair of those who cook, whether in restaurants or at home. Perhaps the most difficult to prepare of all the items in the kitchen's array, they are, at their best, the final wave of the wand which casts an enchantment on whatever comes out of pan or kettle.

At Lüchow's we prepare the best from the French and German cuisines, which between them have produced most of the world's fine sauces. Here one may experience the rich savor of a brown sauce on beef, the opulent and herb-flavored blessing that a burgundy sauce gives to ham, the creamy golden texture of Hollandaise Sauce served with fish, and our own Vinaigrette Sauce which, with mixed greens, head cheese, and chopped hard-cooked egg, makes a very special appetizer.

A meal interlaced with the subtle flavoring of sauces is a testimonial to the artistry of any kitchen. At Lüchow's the testimonial begins with the tangy crimson Cocktail Sauce on your shrimp, and continues to the delicious Preisselbeeren which is served with the traditional German pancake.

BÉCHAMEL SAUCE

⅓ *cup butter*
½ *medium-size onion, minced*
⅓ *cup flour*
3 *cups hot milk*
1 *teaspoon salt*
¼ *teaspoon pepper*
2 *sprigs parsley*
¼ *teaspoon grated nutmeg*

Melt butter in saucepan; add onion and cook until very light brown. Stir flour in smoothly; cook a few minutes longer. Gradually add milk and seasonings and stir well. Cook slowly 25 to 30 minutes, stirring gently but steadily until sauce is thick and smooth. If sauce must stand, stir occasionally to prevent film from forming on top. Makes about 3 cups sauce.

CREAM SAUCE

2 *cups Béchamel Sauce* (*see recipe*)
1 *cup top milk or cream*
½ *tablespoon lemon juice*

Cook Béchamel Sauce until reduced to about 1 cup. Add milk or cream and lemon juice. Cook, stirring constantly, until ready to boil; remove from heat. Makes about 3 cups.

MUSHROOM SAUCE

1½ *cups Cream Sauce* (*see recipe*)
½ *cup sliced fresh or canned mushrooms*
1 *tablespoon butter*

Make Cream Sauce. Sauté mushrooms in butter 5 minutes. Add to Cream Sauce. Mix and serve. Makes about 2 cups sauce.

MUSTARD SAUCE FOR BROILED FISH

1 teaspoon English mustard
3 tablespoons white wine
1 cup Cream Sauce (see recipe)

Mix mustard and wine smoothly together; stir into hot Cream Sauce. Serve on broiled fish. Makes about 1 cup; serves 4 or more.

BROWN SAUCE

⅓ cup beef suet
1 onion, chopped
1 carrot, diced
⅓ cup flour
1½ cups stock or bouillon
1 cup canned tomatoes (3 fresh tomatoes)
1½ cups red wine
2 sprigs parsley
1 stalk celery, chopped
1 bay leaf
¼ teaspoon thyme
1 clove garlic
½ teaspoon salt
3 or 4 peppercorns

Melt suet; cook onion and carrot 3 or 4 minutes. Add flour; stir and cook until browned. Add stock, tomatoes, and wine. Bring to a boil, stirring continually until flour and fat are well mixed with liquid. Add herbs, garlic, salt, and peppercorns; reduce heat and cook gently. Skim when necessary. After 2 hours the sauce should be well cooked down. Strain; use as called for in recipes. Makes 2 cups.

BURGUNDY SAUCE FOR HAM

1 small onion, chopped fine
1 cup burgundy wine
1 tablespoon currant jelly
1 bay leaf
½ teaspoon thyme
1 teaspoon minced parsley

½ cup Brown Sauce (see recipe)
1 tablespoon butter

Heat onion, wine, currant jelly, and herbs together. Cook slowly until liquid is reduced a little. Add Brown Sauce; boil until slightly thickened. Strain; add butter. Makes about 1¼ cups.

CAPER SAUCE

3 tablespoons butter
3 tablespoons flour
½ teaspoon salt
½ teaspoon Worcestershire or A1 sauce
2 cups stock or bouillon
1 tablespoon capers

Melt butter; stir flour smoothly into it. Add salt and Worcestershire or A1 sauce. Slowly stirring, add stock or bouillon. When smooth and thickened, add capers. Serve on Hash à la Lübeck or in other recipes as directed. Makes a little more than 2 cups; serves 4 to 6.

Anchovy Cream Sauce: Substitute chopped anchovy fillets for capers.

COCKTAIL SAUCE
FOR SHRIMPS, CRAB MEAT, ETC.

1 cup chili sauce
1 cup ketchup
½ cup freshly grated horseradish
Dash of Tabasco sauce

Mix well together. Serve on chilled sea food. Makes 2½ cups; serves 12 or more.

DILL SAUCE À LA CHARLES PICKEL
FOR FISH

> *2 egg yolks*
> *1 ounce wine vinegar*
> *1 ounce white wine*
> *Seasonings (very little), consisting of salt, pepper,*
>   *English mustard, ground whole spice, lemon juice,*
>   *sugar*
> *6 ounces olive oil*
> *Chopped dill*

Beat egg yolks with vinegar, wine, and seasonings. Add the oil very slowly. Finish with chopped fresh dill. Makes about 1 cup.

LÜCHOW'S VINAIGRETTE SAUCE

> *3 ounces calf's brain (½ brain)*
> *⅓ cup vinegar*
> *½ teaspoon salt*
> *½ teaspoon pepper*
> *1 tablespoon English mustard*
> *1 tablespoon sugar*
> *½ cup salad oil*
> *¼ cup finely chopped chives, onions, and pickles*
> *2 hard-cooked eggs, chopped fine*

Wash calf's brain in cold water; drain. Remove arteries and membranes; cover with cold water; let stand 1 hour. Drain. Place in kettle; cover with water containing ½ tablespoon vinegar. Cook slowly 15 to 20 minutes; drain. Pour cold water over brain; drain; press through sieve.

Mix dry ingredients and season brain. Stir oil and remaining vinegar alternately into the mixture until consistency is smooth and like mayonnaise. Beat mixed greens into it. Spoon onto sliced head cheese; sprinkle liberally with chopped hard-cooked egg. Serve as appetizer. Serves 8.

HOLLANDAISE SAUCE

3 egg yolks
1 tablespoon water
½ pound butter, melted
½ teaspoon salt
1 tablespoon hot water
1 tablespoon lemon juice

Place eggs and water in upper part of double boiler over hot, but not boiling, water. Do not let water boil; keep it just below that temperature. Stir eggs and water briskly with a wire whip until creamy. Add butter slowly and continue to stir steadily. Be sure butter is smoothly combined after each addition. Add 1 tablespoon hot water to make sauce lighter.

When the sauce is to be served with fish, add lemon juice with the hot water. Makes about 2 cups.

HORSERADISH SAUCE

3 tablespoons butter
3 tablespoons flour
1 cup hot milk
½ cup beef stock
¼ teaspoon grated nutmeg
1 tablespoon white vinegar
½ teaspoon salt
¼ teaspoon white pepper
½ cup freshly grated horseradish

Melt butter; stir flour smoothly into it. Add hot milk and stock;

stir and cook until well blended. Add nutmeg, vinegar, salt, and pepper; mix well. Stir continually until smooth and thickened. Strain through sieve; beat horseradish in just before serving. Makes about 1¾ cups; serves 8 to 10.

MUSTARD SAUCE

> ½ *onion, chopped*
> ¼ *pound butter*
> 2 *tablespoons flour*
> ½ *cup white wine*
> 2 *cups beef or veal broth or stock*
> 2 *teaspoons English mustard*

Cook onion in butter a few minutes. Blend in flour and stir until evenly mixed. Add wine and stock and stir until smooth. Simmer 10 minutes, stirring frequently. Add mustard and stir until smoothly mixed. Makes about 3 cups sauce.

PAPRIKA SAUCE

> 2 *shallots, chopped*
> 1 *clove garlic, chopped*
> 1 *tablespoon butter*
> 2 *tablespoons flour*
> 1 *tablespoon paprika*
> 2 *cups stock or bouillon*
> ½ *cup dry white wine*
> 2 *tablespoons sour cream*
> *Lemon juice (optional)*

Sauté shallots and garlic in butter 5 minutes. Stir flour and paprika in smoothly; blend well. Add stock and wine, stirring continually. Cook over low heat, stirring, until thickened, about 15 minutes. Add sour cream. If not sufficiently tart, add lemon juice. Mix. Makes 2½ cups.

SOUR CREAM SAUCE

> *2 shallots, chopped*
> *4 tablespoons butter*
> *2 tablespoons flour*
> *2 cups stock or bouillon*
> *½ cup white wine*
> *2 tablespoons sour cream*
> *Lemon juice (optional)*

Sauté shallots in butter 5 minutes; stir flour in smoothly; blend well. Add stock and wine, stirring continually. Cook over low heat and stir until thickened, about 15 minutes. Add sour cream. If not sufficiently tart, add lemon juice. Mix. Serve with Brochette of Pork Tenderloin and other dishes. Makes about 2½ cups.

TOMATO SAUCE

> *2 tablespoons butter*
> *1 carrot, chopped*
> *1 small onion, chopped*
> *4 tablespoons flour*
> *3 or 4 fresh tomatoes, peeled and chopped*
> *½ green pepper, chopped*
> *1½ cups stock or bouillon*
> *½ teaspoon salt*
> *¼ teaspoon pepper*
> *1 teaspoon sugar*
> *1 or 2 cloves garlic*
> *½ teaspoon thyme*
> *1 bay leaf, crumbled*

Melt butter; cook carrot and onion until tender. Stir flour in; mix smoothly. Stir and cook until lightly browned. Add tomatoes, green pepper, stock, salt, pepper, sugar, and garlic. Boil, stirring until slightly thickened. Add thyme and bay leaf. Lower heat and cook slowly, about 30 minutes. Strain. Reheat and boil 5 minutes, stirring constantly. Makes about 1¾ cups.

VELOUTÉ SAUCE

> ⅓ *cup butter*
> ⅓ *cup flour*
> 3 *cups stock or bouillon*
> ½ *teaspoon salt*
> 2 *or 3 peppercorns*
> 1 *sprig parsley, minced*
> ¼ *teaspoon grated nutmeg*

Melt butter. Stir flour slowly into it; blend until smooth but not brown. Add stock and cook, stirring continually until flour and butter are smoothly blended with stock. Add salt, peppercorns, and parsley. Reduce heat and cook slowly until reduced to about 2 cups of sauce. Strain. Use as called for in recipes. Makes about 2 cups.

DESSERT SAUCES

CUSTARD SAUCE

> 3 *or 4 egg yolks*
> ¼ *cup sugar*
> ⅛ *teaspoon salt*
> 2 *cups milk*
> 1 *teaspoon sherry*

Beat yolks lightly in upper part of double boiler. Add sugar and salt; mix. Scald milk; add slowly to yolks, stirring continually.

Cook over hot water until custard begins to thicken. Do not boil. Remove from hot water; let cool. Add sherry; mix. Chill thoroughly. Makes about 2¼ cups.

HOT CHOCOLATE SAUCE FOR GERMAN PANCAKES

> *1½ cups sugar*
> *3 tablespoons butter*
> *4 ounces (squares) chocolate, melted*
> *1 cup cream*
> *¼ cup sherry*
> *1 teaspoon vanilla*

Mix sugar, butter, chocolate, and cream in saucepan; stir until dissolved. Heat and let boil without stirring 7 minutes. Stir in sherry and vanilla. Remove from heat; set pan over hot water and keep sauce warm until ready to serve. Makes about 2 cups.

> *Philip Liebmann of Rheingold fame likes the German Pancake with Chocolate Sauce.*

PREISSELBEEREN SAUCE

> *2 quarts fresh Preissel berries*
> *1 pound sugar*
> *Peel of ¼ lemon*
> *Peel of ¼ orange*
> *1 small stick cinnamon (optional)*

Clean berries; add sugar, lemon and orange peels, and cinnamon (optional). Do not add water. Simmer until berries are tender. *Preissel* berries can be obtained fresh or preserved in water in jars. (These berries are red, a little smaller than cranberries and similar in taste and size to lingonberries.)

11.

DESSERTS

Even a Lüchow meal must end at last, but this sadness can be considerably assuaged with a Lüchow dessert. It would be idle to pretend that any one of these delights will do anything at all for dieters. I can only recommend that such unfortunates skip everything else but the entree.

For one should approach the end of the menu with a clear conscience and the prospect of new gustatory enjoyment among the crumb cakes, apple cakes, *Torten,* pies, and the vast German Pancake rolled about a luscious filling.

Possibly, with the imminence of satiety, it might be as well to order something lighter, say our Cheese Cake, or the Linzer Torte, Rote Grütze, with its whipped cream topping, or Mince or Pumpkin Pie, or Strudel.

At luncheon, desserts most often chosen are Schnecken, the various kinds of coffee cake, rice pudding, and apple cake.

But in time you must really try the German Pancake, which is a drama played at your table by two characters, the chef and the waiter, or captain. It is the climax of the Lüchow cuisine, and let us hear no more talk of waistlines. Waiter, please bring us a little champagne, and ask the orchestra to play "The Blue Danube"!

APPLE CRUMB CAKE
APFEL STREUSELKUCHEN

> ½ *cup milk*
> *1 cake compressed yeast*
> *2 tablespoons sugar*
> *1 teaspoon salt*
> *2 eggs, well beaten*
> *Grated peel 1 lemon*
> *2½ cups sifted flour*
> *6 tablespoons melted shortening or butter*
> *2 or 3 ripe apples*

CRUMBS OR STREUSEL:

> *5 ounces almond paste*
> *5 ounces sugar*
> *5 ounces butter*
> *5 ounces flour*
> *Dash of vanilla*

Scald milk; let cool to lukewarm. Dissolve yeast in milk; add sugar and salt and stir. Let stand 5 minutes. Add eggs, lemon peel, and a little flour; mix. Add remaining flour alternately with shortening or butter. Beat well while mixing.

Turn out on lightly floured board. Let stand 10 minutes, then knead well until smooth and elastic. Put dough in greased bowl; cover loosely with folded towel. Let rise in warm, not hot, place.

When double in bulk, punch dough down, place on lightly floured board, and roll out lightly and quickly to about ¼ inch thickness. Place on floured or greased baking sheet. Cover lightly and let rise again till ½ inch thick.

Wash, peel, core apples; slice thin; spread over top of dough.

For Streusel, combine almond paste and sugar; blend well. Add remaining ingredients; blend completely. Place in refrigerator to chill. To form crumbs, grate this chilled mixture.

Sprinkle crumbs thickly over the sliced apples. Bake in moderate oven (350° F.) 35 to 45 minutes. Serves 8.

APPLE PANCAKES
APFEL PFANNKUCHEN

> *German Pancake batter (see recipe)*
> *2 or 3 ripe apples*
> *2 tablespoons butter*
> *Sugar*
> *Powdered cinnamon*

Make pancake batter as in German Pancake recipe.

Wash apples; peel, core, and slice thin.

Melt enough butter in large frying pan to coat bottom and sides; pour very thin coating of batter in pan (2 or 3 tablespoons). Tilt pan to spread batter; let bake about 1 minute.

Cover pancake with apples. Pour 2 or 3 tablespoons batter over apples. Turn cake with wide pancake turner when browned on bottom; brown other side. Fold over like omelet or roll loosely. Cut in half. Dash with sugar and cinnamon. Serves 2.

> *At Lüchow's an order of a German Pancake for dessert for two calls for a spectacular performance on the part of the chef and the waiter, or captain, who is in charge of your table. The pancake, when borne from the kitchen, measures about a foot and a half in diameter. It is delicately browned, hot, ready for the ministrations of the captain.*
>
> *Working swiftly at a serving table at your elbow, he sprinkles the top of the pancake thickly with sugar and powdered cinnamon from huge glass shakers. He quickly squeezes the juice of lemon over this and then spreads the famous imported Preisselbeeren (lingonberries) or huckleberries, cooked apples, or chocolate sauce thickly over the sugared surface and rolls the cake like a jelly roll.*

Next he cuts the roll in 2 pieces, sprinkles them with more sugar and cinnamon, and slips each onto a plate. If you like, he will sprinkle these rolls with Jamaica rum or kirschwasser, ignite it, and then place this succulent dessert before you while the sugary flames are dancing across its surface.

The chef's pan for this mammoth pancake is a large, long-handled thin iron frying pan. Each cake is made with 4 or more tablespoons of batter poured into the heated pan, which has been generously buttered. The batter must be spread quickly to form a large, thin pancake. As soon as it bubbles and the bottom is set, it is turned with a wide pancake turner and baked on the other side.

Here is his recipe:

LÜCHOW'S GERMAN PANCAKE
PFANNKUCHEN

6 eggs
1½ cups sifted flour
¼ teaspoon salt
1 tablespoon sugar
1 pint milk
½ pound butter
Powdered cinnamon in shaker
Sugar in shaker
Juice 1 lemon
Preisselbeeren, *huckleberry jam, cooked apples,*
    or chocolate sauce
Jamaica rum, kirschwasser (*optional*)

Beat eggs lightly; beat in flour, salt, and sugar, then milk. Beat 5 minutes in all. The batter should be thin and smooth.

Melt enough butter in a wide frying pan to coat bottom and sides. When hot, pour in 4 to 5 tablespoons batter. Turn and slant pan to make batter spread to form large, thin flat pancake. Cook until batter bubbles; turn; bake other side. Slip onto hot plate. Makes 4 to 6 pancakes.

A wine you will enjoy with this dessert is a Château Yquem.

APPLE FRITTERS WITH WINE FOAM

> *3 medium-size apples*
> *¼ cup white wine*
> *½ cup sugar*
> *¼ teaspoon powdered cinnamon*
> *3 eggs*
> *1 cup sifted flour*
> *¼ teaspoon baking powder*
> *¼ teaspoon salt*
> *½ cup milk*
> *3 tablespoons butter*

Wash, peel, core apples. Cut in thick slices. Mix wine, sugar, baking powder, and cinnamon and pour over apples. Cover; let stand 1 hour.

When ready to cook, mix batter by beating eggs, flour, salt, and milk smoothly together. Dip apples in batter and sauté in hot butter until almost set. Top each with more batter; let cook until browned on both sides. Drain on thick paper toweling on pan in warm oven. Leave oven door open.

Serve with Wine Foam. Serves 6.

WINE FOAM:

> *8 eggs, separated*
> *1 cup confectioners' sugar*
> *½ cup madeira*
> *Pinch of salt*

Beat yolks and sugar in upper part of double boiler over hot, but not boiling, water. When slightly thickened and foamy, gradually add wine; continue to beat sauce until it doubles in

bulk and begins to thicken. (Do not let water boil under it.)
Whip egg white stiff; add salt. Fold into Wine Foam. Serve
on fritters. Serves 6.

STEWED APPLES IN BUTTER AND WHITE WINE

> *6 apples*
> *3 tablespoons butter*
> *½ cup white wine*
> *½ cup water*
> *1 cup sugar*
> *1-inch piece cinnamon stick*
> *1 tablespoon lemon juice*
> *1 tablespoon grated lemon peel*

Wash, peel, and core apples. Cut in thick slices. Sauté lightly in
butter 3 to 5 minutes in saucepan.

Boil wine, water, sugar, cinnamon, lemon juice, and peel 5
minutes. Pour over apples. Cook uncovered until apples are
tender. Pour into serving dish. Serve warm or cold. Serves 6.

APPLE STRUDEL
APFEL STRUDEL

> *2 eggs*
> *6 tablespoons butter*
> *1 cup sifted flour*
> *¼ teaspoon salt*
> *4 medium-size apples*
> *½ cup chopped blanched almonds*
> *2 tablespoons finely chopped citron*
> *¼ cup dried currants*
> *½ cup sugar*
> *1½ teaspoons powdered cinnamon*

Beat eggs with 3 tablespoons softened butter; gradually beat in flour and salt. Knead dough 20 minutes. Stretch out to transparent thinness.

Wash, peel, and core apples. Dice fruit fine and arrange along one side of dough. Scatter almonds and citron over apples. Wash and drain currants and add. Sprinkle with sugar and cinnamon. Dot with 1 tablespoon butter.

Fold pastry over filling; shape in long roll. Place in long, lightly greased pan. Spread remaining butter over top.

Bake in hot oven (400° F.) until pastry is golden, about 30 minutes. Reduce heat to 350° F. and continue baking until well browned. Serve warm, with or without whipped cream. Serves 4 to 6.

COFFEE CAKE
BUNDKUCHEN OR GUGELHUPF

> *1 ounce-cake compressed yeast*
> *1 cup lukewarm milk*
> *6 cups sifted flour*
> *1 cup seedless raisins*
> *½ cup dried currants*
> *¾ cup sugar*
> *1 cup butter*
> *8 eggs*
> *1 tablespoon cognac or rum*
> *½ teaspoon salt*
> *1 tablespoon grated lemon peel*
> *½ cup chopped blanched almonds*
> *3 tablespoons confectioners' sugar*
> *3 tablespoons powdered cinnamon*

Dissolve yeast in milk; beat in 1 cup flour. Cover bowl loosely with folded towel. Let stand in warm room to rise, 1½ hours.

Wash raisins and currants; drain. Let soak a few minutes in clean water.

Beat sugar and butter together until light and fluffy. Beat in eggs 1 at a time. Add cognac or rum, and salt. Add yeast sponge and remaining flour and mix smoothly. Add lemon peel, drained raisins and currants. Mix well, then beat until smooth and elastic.

Place half of dough in greased 9-inch tube pan. Sprinkle with almonds; cover with remaining dough. Cover pan loosely with folded towel; let stand in warm, not hot, place to rise 1½ hours. Sprinkle with confectioners' sugar and cinnamon. Bake in moderate oven (350° F.) 45 minutes to 1 hour. Let cool. Serves 6 to 8.

CHRISTMAS STOLLEN
WEIHNACHTS STOLLEN; ALSO KNOWN AS DRESDENER STOLLEN

> 11 cups sifted flour
> 2 cups milk
> 1¼ cups butter, melted
> 6 eggs
> 1 pound seedless raisins
> 1 pound currants
> ¾ cup sugar
> ½ teaspoon mace
> 1 tablespoon grated lemon peel
> 3 tablespoons lemon juice
> 1 tablespoon cognac
> ¼ pound blanched almonds, chopped
> ½ pound finely chopped citron
> ½ teaspoon salt
> 2 1-ounce cakes compressed yeast, dissolved in
> ½ cup lukewarm water
> ½ teaspoon grated nutmeg

TOPPING:

> ¼ cup butter, melted
> 2 tablespoons cognac
> ½ cup confectioners' sugar

Sift flour into large mixing bowl. Make a hollow in the center and work milk, butter, and eggs in until almost all is mixed.

Wash and drain raisins and currants. Soak a few minutes. Drain and combine with other ingredients. Work all into the dough by hand until evenly mixed. Dough should be stiff.

Beat and fold dough over on itself repeatedly until smooth and all ingredients are evenly distributed. Cover bowl lightly with folded towel. Let set stand in warm, not hot, place 12 hours.

Turn dough out on lightly floured board. Pull in half. Shape each half into a loaf with slightly pointed ends. Place in greased baking pans. Cover lightly with folded towel and let stand in warm, not hot, place until risen to double in bulk.

Bake in moderate oven (350° F.) about 1 hour. While still warm, spread with melted butter and sprinkle with cognac and confectioners' sugar. Makes 2 loaves; serves 16.

FILLED BERLINER PANCAKES OR DOUGHNUTS
FASTNACHT KRAPFEN

> *1 cup milk*
> *1 ounce cake compressed yeast*
> *4½ cups sifted flour*
> *½ cup butter, melted*
> *⅔ cup sugar*
> *½ lemon peel, grated*
> *5 egg yolks, beaten*
> *Flour*
> *Currant jelly or thick cooked apples*
> *Lard or shortening for deep frying*
> *Extra sugar*

Heat milk to lukewarm. Soften yeast in ¼ cup warm milk. Stir 2½ cups flour smoothly into rest of warm milk. Mix yeast quickly into this batter. Cover lightly with folded towel and let stand 1 hour or longer.

After sponge has risen well, mix in melted butter, sugar, lemon peel, egg yolks, and remaining flour. Stir well.

Turn dough out on lightly floured board. Fold over, then roll lightly to ½-inch thickness. Cut with 3-inch round cooky cutter. Spread half of the rounds with 1 heaping teaspoon jelly or cooked apples. Cover these with remaining rounds. Crimp edges firmly together with fingers. Leave on floured board. Cover lightly with folded towel and let rise in warm room ½ hour, or until light and puffy.

Fry a few Berliners at a time in deep hot fat (360° F.) until golden brown. Remove from fat; drain on thick paper toweling. While hot, roll in sugar. Makes 1½ to 2 dozen.

FRUIT FRITTERS

> ⅔ *cup sifted flour*
> ¾ *teaspoon baking powder*
> ¼ *teaspoon salt*
> ¼ *cup white wine*
> 4 *tablespoons melted butter*
> 2 *eggs, separated*
> ½ *teaspoon vanilla extract or cognac*
> 1 *cup sugared raw fruit, such as sliced peaches,*
> *apricots, cherries, apples, or bananas*
> *Fat for deep frying*
> *Confectioners' sugar*

Sift flour, baking powder, and salt. Beat wine and butter into flour mixture. Beat egg yolks slightly and add. Whip egg whites stiff. Add flavoring or cognac to batter; fold in egg whites.

Stir sugared fruit into batter. Drop by spoonfuls into deep hot fat (365° F. to 375° F.). Fry 2 to 5 minutes. Drain on thick paper toweling. Sift confectioners' sugar over before serving. Serves 4.

OMELET SOUFFLÉ

> *5 tablespoons sugar*
> *3 egg yolks*
> *Pinch of grated lemon rind*
> *6 egg whites*
> *Butter for baking dish*
> *Powdered sugar*

Beat sugar and yolks together until light and creamy; add grated lemon rind. Beat whites stiff; fold into yolk mixture. Pour into buttered shallow baking dish. Shape with spatula in oval-shaped mound. Make shallow depression through center with spoon. Bake in moderate oven (375° F.) 18 to 20 minutes. Sprinkle with powdered sugar a few minutes before removing from oven. Serve at once. Serves 2 to 3.

Hot Chocolate Sauce or Custard Sauce may be served with Omelet Soufflé.

PASTRY SNAILS
SCHNECKEN

> *2 cups milk*
> *8 cups flour*
> *1 cake yeast (compressed)*
> *6 ounces butter, melted*
> *½ cup sugar*
> *6 eggs, beaten*

FILLING:

> *1 cup brown sugar*
> *1 tablespoon powdered cinnamon*
> *½ cup dried currants*
> *½ cup chopped blanched almonds*

½ *cup butter, melted*
Granulated sugar

Heat milk to lukewarm; stir 2¼ cups flour smoothly into all but
¼ cup of the milk. Soften yeast in the ¼ cup milk, then beat
into flour and milk mixture to make a light sponge. Cover loosely
with folded towel and let rise in warm, but not hot, place until
double in bulk. Then beat in butter, sugar, peel, eggs, and remaining flour; mix thoroughly. Add more flour if needed. Place
in refrigerator for approximately 8 hours.

Roll out lightly on lightly floured board to 1-inch thickness.

Sprinkle with sugar, cinnamon, washed and drained currants,
and almonds. Add generous sprinkling of melted butter; roll up
carefully. Cut crosswise in 1-inch slices. Place in floured or
lightly greased baking pan. Cover lightly with folded towel and
let rise in warm, not hot, place 30 minutes.

Bake in hot oven (425° F.) 25 minutes, or until pastry is
golden. Brush while hot with remaining melted butter and
sprinkle lightly with sugar. Makes 10 Schnecken.

RASPBERRY PUDDING
ROTE GRÜTZE

> *1 quart juice from cold-pack raspberries*
> ⅔ *cup granulated sugar*
> *2 pieces lemon peel, about 1 inch long*
> *1 pint red wine, claret type*
> *2 cups water*
> ¾ *cup minute tapioca*
> *1 cup heavy cream*
> ¼ *cup powdered sugar*

Place juice in enamel kettle; sprinkle with sugar. Add peel,
wine, and water. Bring to a boil and cook 10 minutes. Let cool;

strain through fine sieve. Reheat juice. Add tapioca and cook, stirring continually, until clear, about 5 minutes. Pour into glass dessert dishes; fill about ⅘ full. Chill.

Whip cream, gradually adding sugar, and decorate top of each dish. Serves 6 to 8.

LÜCHOW'S CHEESE CAKE

> *Kuchen dough*
> *6 ounces butter*
> *2 cups sugar*
> *½ cup cornstarch*
> *¼ teaspoon salt*
> *10 eggs*
> *2½ pounds baker's cheese or pot cheese (not cottage cheese)*
> *1 tablespoon grated lemon peel*
> *1 teaspoon vanilla*
> *3 cups milk*
> *3 cups heavy cream (not whipped)*

Prepare Kuchen dough proportionately and line bottom and sides of 12-inch spring-form cake pan. Use hand or wooden spoon to make smooth, even lining. Mix butter, sugar, cornstarch, salt, and eggs. When thoroughly mixed, add cheese, grated lemon peel, and vanilla. Add milk and cream. Pour into cake pan.

Bake in moderate oven (350° F.) about 1 hour. When done, turn off heat; let cake remain in oven ½ hour longer, until cooled. Serves 12.

RASPBERRY TART
HIMBEER KUCHEN

> *1½ cups sifted flour*
> *¼ teaspoon salt*
> *¾ cup sugar*
> *1½ teaspoons powdered cinnamon*
> *½ cup butter*
> *2 eggs, beaten*
> *1½ quarts raspberries*
> *1 teaspoon cornstarch*
> *2 eggs, beaten*
> *½ cup heavy cream*

Sift flour, salt, 1½ tablespoons sugar, and cinnamon together. Beat butter until creamy; combine with flour mixture to make smooth dough. Add 2 beaten eggs; mix well.

Chill dough 1 or 2 hours. Roll out to ⅛-inch thickness or spread with wooden spoon in 8-inch greased layer-cake pan. Cover bottom and sides with pastry; crimp decorative edge around top. Bake in hot oven (450° F.) 15 minutes.

Wash berries; drain. Add remaining sugar. Spread berries in baked shell; save the little raspberry juice which remains in bowl. Return tart to oven and reduce heat to moderate (375° F.). Bake 10 minutes. Let cool.

Mix 1 teaspoon water and cornstarch; add to eggs and mix; add cream. Cook and stir in top of double boiler over hot water until custard is thickened. Pour over the slightly cooled tart. Let cool. Serves 6.

Fresh Blueberry Tart (or Cake) (Beeren Kuchen): Substitute blueberries for raspberries in the above recipe.

RICE PUDDING

> 1 cup rice
> 2½ cups milk
> ⅓ cup seedless raisins
> 1 cup milk
> ½ cup cream
> ⅛ teaspoon salt
> 3½ tablespoons sugar
> 1 tablespoon butter
> 1 teaspoon vanilla
> 2 eggs
> ½ teaspoon grated lemon peel
> 1 teaspoon lemon juice
> 1 cup whipped cream

Wash rice; drain. Cover with 2½ cups milk; cook covered until rice is fluffy and soft and milk is absorbed. Strain in colander; rinse with cold water; drain. Wash raisins; drain. Cover with water and let stand 15 minutes or longer. Drain.

Mix 1 cup milk, cream, salt, sugar, butter, vanilla, and eggs. Combine with rice. Add raisins, lemon peel, and juice. Mix lightly. Pour into greased baking dish. Set dish in shallow pan of hot water. Bake in moderate oven (325° F.) until set.

Cover with whipped cream; sprinkle lightly with mixture of equal portions of sugar and cinnamon. Brown top quickly. Serve warm or cold. Serves 6.

PIES

PASTRY FOR PIES AND TARTS

> 1½ cups sifted flour
> ½ teaspoon salt

½ *cup lard or shortening*
4 *to 5 tablespoons cold water*

Sift flour with salt. Add fat; cut in with pastry blender or blending fork until pieces are small as marbles. Add cold water by teaspoonfuls, mixing lightly with fork until all pieces are barely dampened.

Turn mixture on waxed paper and press lightly and quickly into ball. Cut dough in half and roll each half in waxed paper. Chill slightly in refrigerator before rolling.

Roll pastry ⅛ inch thick, rolling lightly from center to outer edges. Line pie pan; trim edge. If it is to be baked as a shell, crimp decorative rim around edge.

For covered pie, leave edge until pie is filled. With upper layer of pastry or pastry strips in place, crimp top or strips and lower pastry together by pressing with tines of fork or fingers. Makes pastry for 8- or 9-inch 2-crust pie.

Filling: Delicious fillings for pie shells are stewed fruit topped with sweetened whipped cream: apricots, damson plums, gooseberries, tart cherries, strawberries, huckleberries, etc.

PUMPKIN PIE

Pastry for 8-inch pie (*see recipe*)
1½ *cups mashed, cooked* (*or canned*) *pumpkin*
6 *eggs, separated*
⅓ *cup brown sugar*
¼ *teaspoon powdered ginger*
¼ *teaspoon powdered cinnamon*
2½ *cups milk*
½ *cup molasses*
¼ *teaspoon salt*

Line pie pan with pastry; crimp decorative rim around edge.
Beat pumpkin, egg yolks, sugar, spices, milk, and molasses.

Add salt to egg whites; whip stiff and fold into pumpkin mixture. Fill pie shell.

Bake in hot oven (450° F.) 15 minutes; lower heat to moderate (325° F.) and bake 30 minutes longer. Serves 5 or 6.

COCONUT CREAM PIE

> *1 baked pie shell (see Pastry recipe)*
> *3 egg yolks*
> *⅓ cup sugar*
> *¼ teaspoon salt*
> *2½ tablespoons cornstarch*
> *1 tablespoon butter*
> *2 cups milk, scalded*
> *1 teaspoon rum*
> *1 cup grated fresh coconut*

Beat yolks. Add sugar gradually, then salt, cornstarch, and butter. Place in top of double boiler over hot water. Stir scalded milk into egg mixture. Stir constantly until thickened. Let cool. Add coconut and flavoring.

Pour into baked pie shell. Cover with meringue. Bake in slow oven (300° F.) 15 to 20 minutes. Serves 5 or 6.

MERINGUE FOR THIS PIE:

> *3 egg whites*
> *⅛ teaspoon salt*
> *¼ teaspoon cream of tartar*
> *4 tablespoons granulated sugar*
> *½ cup grated fresh coconut*
> *½ teaspoon vanilla*

Beat egg whites on a platter. Whip until frothy; add salt and cream of tartar and continue whipping until stiff. Beat sugar and coconut in a little at a time. Beat in vanilla. Spread thickly over pie and bake as directed.

MINCE PIE

> *Pastry for 2-crust pie (see recipe)*
> *2 cups mincemeat*
> *2 tablespoons cognac*

MINCEMEAT:

> *1 pound beef*
> *½ pound suet*
> *2 pounds tart apples*
> *1 pound dried currants*
> *1 pound seedless raisins*
> *1 cup cider*
> *¼ pound citron, chopped*
> *½ teaspoon powdered cinnamon*
> *½ teaspoon powdered cloves*
> *½ teaspoon pepper*
> *½ teaspoon grated nutmeg*
> *½ teaspoon salt*
> *Juice and grated peel 1 lemon*
> *Juice and grated peel 1 orange*
> *1 cup cognac or whisky*

Wipe meat with damp cloth; cover with water and cook slowly, covered, until tender, about 3 hours. Let cool.

Wash, peel, and core apples. Wash currants and raisins; drain. Cover with a little cold water and let soak 30 minutes; drain. Put meat through food chopper with apples, suet, currants, and raisins. Add remaining ingredients except liquor. Mix thoroughly. Cook slowly 1 hour. After first 30 minutes add cognac or whisky. Let cool and use, or seal at once in sterile jars. Makes about 2 quarts. Use 2 cups for each 8-inch pie.

Roll pastry about ¼ inch thick; line pie pan; trim edge. Fill with mincemeat. Cover top with pastry; trim edge; press edge of upper and lower crusts together with tines of fork or with fingers and crimp in decorative rim. Gash top crust in 2 or 3 decorative cuttings. Bake in hot oven (400° F.) 25 minutes; lower heat to moderate (325° F.) and bake 15 to 20 minutes longer, until crust is golden and done. Serves 6.

KUCHEN DOUGH

This dough is used for German apple, plum, peach, and other fruit "cakes" or Kuchen.

5 cups sifted flour
½ teaspoon salt
¾ cup sugar
6 ounces butter
½ teaspoon mace
Grated rind 2 lemons
4 eggs, beaten
1 cup milk
½ ounce yeast

FILLING:

Peeled, sliced fruit
Light brown sugar
Powdered cinnamon
Butter

Sift flour, salt, and sugar together. Work butter and grated lemon rind smoothly into this with wooden spoon. Beat in eggs and add milk, in which yeast has been dissolved. With spoon spread dough on bottom and sides of lightly greased round cake pan, spring-form pan, or ovenproof dish. Crimp decorative rim around top. Makes dough for 1 cake.

Apple Cake; Peach Cake; Berry Cake: Fill lined pan with peeled and sliced fruit. Sprinkle generously with sugar and cinnamon; dot with butter. Bake in a hot oven (425° F.) about 25 minutes. Serves 4 to 6.

TORTEN

ALMOND TORTE
MANDELTORTE

> *1 cup sugar*
> *6 eggs, separated*
> *Grated peel and juice 1 lemon*
> *1 teaspoon powdered cinnamon*
> *1 cup ground unblanched almonds*
> *½ to 1 cup toasted bread crumbs*
> *¼ teaspoon salt*
> *Chocolate Butter Cream Icing*

Beat sugar into egg yolks until smooth, light, and fluffy. Add lemon peel and juice, cinnamon, almonds, and enough crumbs to make light batter. Mix well. Whip egg whites stiff; fold into batter. Bake in greased 8-inch tube pan in moderate oven (350° F.) about 1 hour. Let cool in pan. Cover with Chocolate (or Mocha) Butter Cream Icing. Serves 6.

CHOCOLATE BUTTER CREAM ICING:

> *2 ounces (squares) chocolate*
> *3 tablespoons butter*
> *¼ cup heavy cream*
> *⅛ teaspoon salt*
> *1 teaspoon vanilla or rum flavoring*
> *2 cups confectioners' sugar*

Melt chocolate over hot water; stir butter into it. Heat cream slightly; add with salt and mix. Remove from heat. Let cool. Add flavoring and beat sugar in gradually. When smooth and good consistency for spreading, use on top of Almond Torte.

Mocha Butter Cream Icing: Substitute 3 tablespoons strong, freshly made coffee for chocolate in above recipe.

HAZELNUT TORTE

NUSSTORTE

> *This is the Lüchow dessert which makes famous actresses go off their reducing diets and is a favorite of men as well as women; one of the most delectable of all the old-time German* Torten *for which this restaurant has been famous during the seventy years of its existence.*
>
> *To make it, start with this special cake:*

½ *pound (1 cup) granulated sugar*
9 *eggs*
½ *pound sifted cake flour*
½ *cup butter, melted*
1 *teaspoon vanilla*

Mix together sugar and eggs which have been well beaten. Fold in flour. When it is about half finished, add the melted butter, then mix well together. Add vanilla. Pour into lightly greased spongecake form. Bake in slow oven (325° F.) about 45 minutes. Let cool on cake rack. Slice in 3 layers.

FILLING:

¾ *pound shelled hazelnuts*
1½ *pints heavy cream*
¾ *cup granulated sugar*
1 *teaspoon vanilla*

Spread hazelnuts in pan and toast for about ½ hour in 300° F. oven. Rub skins off the hazelnuts, and then grind medium-fine.

Whip cream; combine with nuts and sugar. Spread between cake layers.

TOPPING:

> ½ *pound (1¾ cups) 4X sugar*
> *3 or 4 tablespoons water*
> ¼ *pound (1 cup) shelled hazelnuts*

Mix sugar and water together smoothly. Spread over top and sides of *Torte*. Toast nuts, remove skins, and grind (see above). Sprinkle on sides and decorate top with toasted nuts. Serves 6 to 8.

LINZER TORTE

> *1 cup butter*
> *1 cup sugar*
> *1 teaspoon grated lemon peel*
> *2 eggs*
> *1½ cups sifted flour*
> *1 cup unblanched almonds, ground*
> ½ *teaspoon powdered cinnamon*
> ½ *teaspoon powdered cloves*
> *1 tablespoon cocoa*
> ¼ *teaspoon salt*
> *Raspberry jam or apple butter*

Beat butter and sugar together until creamy. Add lemon peel. Beat eggs in 1 at a time. Gradually add flour, almonds, spices, cocoa, and salt. Beat until thoroughly blended and smooth. If dough is very soft, chill.

Roll to ¼-inch thickness between sheets of waxed paper, then line shallow casserole or pie dish. Crimp decorative edge around top. Fill dish almost to top with raspberry jam or apple butter.

Roll remaining dough, cut in strips about ¾-inch wide. Make a lattice over the preserves. Trim ends of strips and crimp to *Torte* edge. Bake in slow oven (300° F.) 1 hour. Serves 6.

SAND TORTE

5 whole eggs
5 egg yolks
1½ cups sugar
Grated peel of 1 lemon
4½ ounces sifted flour
4½ ounces cornstarch
9 ounces melted butter

Beat together the whole eggs and egg yolks. Warm up slightly. Add sugar and mix with eggs until mixture is quite stiff. Add lemon peel. Stir in flour and cornstarch, which have been mixed together. Add melted butter. Mix together lightly.

Bake in greased 9-inch tube pan in slow oven (250° F.) about 40 to 45 minutes. Serves 8 or more.

CHERRY TORTE, BLACK FOREST STYLE

1 quart large black cherries
½ cup kirsch
1½ pounds (5 cups) confectioners' sugar
3 tablespoons cornstarch
½ pound butter
3 egg yolks
2 8-inch spongecake layers, 1 inch thick
1 cup finely shaved bittersweet chocolate

Wash cherries; remove stems and seeds. Mix kirsch and 1 cup sugar and pour over fruit in bowl. Let stand at least 2 hours,

then heat to boiling. Mix cornstarch with about 2 tablespoons cherry juice and stir into cherries. Cook and stir until slightly thickened. Remove from heat and let cool. This should be consistency of thin jelly.

Beat butter and remaining sugar smoothly together. Beat egg yolks into this and continue beating until mixture is light and fluffy.

Place layer of cake on plate; make border around edge with butter mixture and spread some butter cream in circle in center of cake. Spread cooled, thickened cherry mixture between butter cream border and center. Place second layer on top; press down just sufficiently to make layers stick together. Cover top and sides of both layers with remaining butter cream. Sprinkle top with chocolate. Serves 6 to 8.

KAISERSCHMARRN

> *German Pancake batter*
> *½ cup dry blanched raisins*
> *2 tablespoons butter*
> *Sugar*
> *Cinnamon*

Melt butter in frying pan, add raisins, pour over this 3 table-spoons batter. Fry on both sides to golden brown. Cut pancake with fork and spoon (do not use knife) in 1½-inch pieces. Dash with sugar and cinnamon.

THE WINES,
BEER, AND
FESTIVALS
AT Lüchow's

OR *Down Where the Würzburger Flows*

When August Lüchow and his friends first sniffed the
fine Bavarian fragrance of Würzburger Hofbrau and
tasted its benign liquid blessing, they were overjoyed for different reasons. To August the beer was a happy reminder of home,
and to those who had never been fortunate enough to sample
such a brew, the gates to a new gastronomic heaven were thrown
open and they hearkened to the singing of hitherto unheard
choirs.

Loud were the cries of anguish when they were cast out of
this paradise by the advent of the first World War. The long dry
reign of Prohibition following immediately after added to their
parched misery. Then, scarcely had imported beer started flowing once more in the thirties when war ended the supply again,
and it was not until 1950 that Würzburger was at last obtainable.
Meanwhile a whole thirsty generation has slipped by and a new
one, unused to the delights of Würzburger, awaits education.

For the uninitiated, then, this celebrated nectar comes from
Upper Bavaria. It is amber in color (between light and dark),
and its special distinction is its status as the original March beer.
When a shipment arrives, the beer has to rest from its journey
for at least three days in the cooler before it can be served.

Würzburger is the glory of Lüchow's beverage list, but the

restaurant also offers seven different kinds of draught beer and fifteen domestic and imported bottled beers. Every week Lüchow's uses about one hundred barrels of draught beer, which is maintained at a cellar temperature of forty degrees. If a guest wants colder beer, a glass, mug, goblet, stein, or seidel is chilled for him. Imported beer is usually served in big half-liter (pint) stone mugs with covers.

It is not at all uncommon for the older customers to ask for warm beer, and in other days the restaurant had beer warmers—nickel pipes filled with hot water—in the bar. Now the task must be done by more modern methods.

On its way from barrel to consumer, beer can find its way into considerable trouble, a thought which seldom occurs to the drinker who watches the brew foaming effortlessly from the tap. Clean pipes are essential, for instance, and some time ago we had the old coil system taken out because it was so difficult to clean the coils, and the modern Zahn system was substituted. Because different pressures are needed for every type of beer, each draught type has to have its own set of pipes. An old bartender's axiom reads, "The older the beer, the greater the froth," a primary factor in determining the correct amount of pressure for the pipes. Our pressures vary from sixteen to eighteen pounds.

A housewife who is particular about her cleaning would be well pleased with the way we clean our beer pipes. Water is run through them until it is clear, and this is followed by a cleaning solution made especially for us, which remains in the pipes for an hour, after which the water is resumed until it becomes clear once more. As a final touch, the pipes are blown out with fifty pounds of pressure.

The tanks are cleaned by hand, which experience has shown is the most effective method. We test the success of the entire procedure by not drawing beer for three days, then drawing a test beer, which always turns out to be perfect. In less effective systems, the beer will not stand more than twenty-four hours without becoming dark and cloudy.

Bock Beer Festival

Besides the Würzburger, another beer specialty on the Lüchow list is October beer, so called because that is the autumnal moment when it is first drawn in Germany. October beer was also a victim of war and Prohibition, and like Würzburg, it returned to these shores in 1950, where patrons first tasted its strong, tangy flavor at the Venison Festival in November of that year.

About Christmas time the brewers are busy preparing another delight for us, the heavy, dark Christmas Bock, which is poured out of the vats where it has been aging for eight months into barrels which are shipped to us.

At Lüchow's beer enjoys a festival all its own on the calendar of special events, when the first days of March come around and the Bock Beer Festival is celebrated. That, too, was resumed in 1950 after fifteen years, and the enthusiasm for it was unconfined. While the amber herald of spring flowed unceasingly for three evenings, a ten-piece German band played the old songs, just as it did in August Lüchow's time.

As a fitting accompaniment for the revelry, we served the menu that traditionally goes with bock beer, which is bockwurst, liver dumplings Bavarian style, a *Schwabenplatte* consisting of liver sausage, roast ham, and pigs' knuckles, and pheasant on wine kraut.

It was a year of festivals, revivals of the great feasts which made Lüchow's famous, and part of my program to restore the flavor of the old days. There is a Venison Festival in November and a Goose Feast in December, with the superb wines these meats demand brought up from our cellars.

The Goose Feast is enough to start the tears from a grateful gourmet's eyes. It begins with a choice of Lüchow appetizers, including marinated herring; soup made of goose giblets and a barley called Giblet Ecossaisse, and consommé with dumplings; then as a prelude to the main theme, goose ragout and potato dumplings, and at last the roast goose itself, served with stewed apples and cranberries.

Goose is always on the Christmas dinner menu at Lüchow's, along with roast prime ribs of beef, boiled carp, baked ham, leg of hare in sour cream sauce, roast turkey, and in the old days there was also buffalo steak. And I might say that goose lingers on through the Christmas holidays, its rich savor filling the nostrils and the stomach.

For both goose and venison, of course, we have the still burgundy and Rhine wines these meats require. At any time you will find about a thousand bottles of Rhine wine and the same number of Moselles in our cellar, and the warehouses hold at least five times that much, ready for transfer.

We import the good French wines—red Bordeaux, burgundies, sauternes, and fifteen varieties of French champagne—and such specialties as a German champagne known as Schaumwine, madeira, sherries, ports, kirsch, kümmel, and Zwetschgen Wasser, a German cordial made from the pits of plums.

In 1951, again for the first time since 1935, we held the May Wine Festival, amid vine leaves and grapes draped about the restaurant, in tribute to Bacchus, while the German band played the spring music that attends the festival. On the menu there is that seasonal dessert, cabinet pudding with May wine sauce. We take down our May wine bowls, hitherto filled only with history, and fill them with the springlike potion which has been celebrated for centuries along the banks of the Rhine, and continues to be a great delight here at Lüchow's, thousands of miles from its origin.

Again, for those who have never tasted it, May wine is Rhine wine to which has been added an extract of *Waldmeister,* the first plant of the German spring. *Waldmeister,* literally "master of the woods," is called woodruff in English, and is sometimes known, too, as May herb. The shoots are gathered when they are about two inches aboveground and then are tied into bunches and steeped in the previous year's Rhine wine for a few days, imparting their beneficence to it and enriching it with a flavor truly inimitable. The resulting extract is mixed with new Rhine wine in large, gaily decorated May wine bowls in which float succulent wild strawberries.

In the Rhineland, it is a village custom to gather in the wine gardens and drink May wine, singing and dancing to the folk music of the bands. It is, quite naturally, a time for love. Boys and girls walk hand in hand from town to town along the banks of the Rhine, sampling the May wine of each famous vineyard along the river. The older ones are content to stroll through the wine gardens of their own villages.

Mr. Seute and his older colleagues report that wine drinking is regaining some of its former popularity, with a new generation which has had to be educated to its uses as an accompaniment to food. Those who discover it find the Lüchow wine card a fascinating catalogue of French and German imports, vintage wines and champagnes, besides American wine and champagnes, and Chilean, Italian, and Hungarian wines. Add to these the imported and domestic beers, and such staples as scotch, rye, and bourbon, gins, rums, vermouths, apéritifs, brandies, and cordials, and no one will find himself unsatisfied.

But try the May wine. Here is our recipe:

> *6 bunches* Waldmeister, *or woodruff*
> *½ pound powdered sugar*
> *1 cup cognac*
> *4 quarts Moselle or Rhine wine*
> *Ice*
> *2 quarts champagne or charged water*
> *1 cup fresh strawberries*

Wash herbs. Place in large bowl with sugar, cognac, 1 quart Moselle or Rhine wine. Cover bowl; let stand overnight. To serve, strain mixture, pour over ice in a large punch bowl, and add remaining three quarts Moselle or Rhine wine. Add champagne or charged water. Float strawberries in the bowl. Serves 10 to 15.

INDEX